The
Book of
Runic
Astrology

The
Book of
Runic
Astrology

Unlock the
Ancient Power of
Your Cosmic Birth Runes

RICHARD
LISTER

HAY HOUSE

Carlsbad, California • New York City
London • Sydney • New Delhi

Published in the United Kingdom by:
Hay House UK Ltd, The Sixth Floor, Watson House
54 Baker Street, London W1U 7BU
Tel: +44 (0)20 3927 7290; Fax: +44 (0)20 3927 7291
www.hayhouse.co.uk

Published in the United States of America by:
Hay House Inc., PO Box 5100, Carlsbad, CA 92018-5100
Tel: (1) 760 431 7695 or (800) 654 5126
Fax: (1) 760 431 6948 or (800) 650 5115; www.hayhouse.com

Published in Australia by:
Hay House Australia Ltd, 18/36 Ralph St, Alexandria NSW 2015
Tel: (61) 2 9669 4299; Fax: (61) 2 9669 4144; www.hayhouse.com.au

Published in India by:
Hay House Publishers India, Muskaan Complex,
Plot No.3, B-2, Vasant Kunj, New Delhi 110 070
Tel: (91) 11 4176 1620; Fax: (91) 11 4176 1630; www.hayhouse.co.in

Tradepaper ISBN: 978-1-4019-7304-9
E-book ISBN: 978-1-78817-947-8
Audiobook ISBN: 978-1-78817-946-1

Interior illustrations: all runic/astrological symbols © Richard Lister; all other images shutterstock.com

10 9 8 7 6 5 4 3 2 1

Printed in the United States of America

For Lisa.
Without you, this would not work.

Contents

Introduction

As I write this, I'm sitting in an ancient fortified Angevin farmhouse, deep in Aquitaine, southwest France. I'm surrounded by lush green fields and the days are short. The dogs are full of leftovers and the cats are warming themselves by the fire. Sheep are grazing outside the windows and geese are honking at anything they don't like. And from what I can tell, they don't like a lot of things. Like wind, other geese, a fence, the house, me.

My soul takes me back over generations long dead. Past the occupation, the trenches, past the Terror and the time of the aristos. Back along the lines of the English kings, who flow back to the Norman dukes, to the jarls of the north, back to the frozen fjords of Norway, Sweden, Denmark and the Faroes.

The ancient walls that surround me, built by people to keep the descendants of those ancient Norwegian tribes out, are warmed by a fire burning wood that was growing before the United States was even a 'thing'.

I feel the well of the past, the flow of the energy, the frequency of life pulsing and changing with each generation. From republic to kingdom to dukedom to burg people, living, loving, trading and dying in these walls and this land.

The constants over all this time have been the pinpricks of light – the stars. And the star pathways illuminating the worlds below them, affecting those living their lives there in subtle but distinct ways.

Rogue stars predicted massive change – the Norman invasion of England was preceded by Halley's comet, for example. Energy changed with equinoxes and solstices. We who walk this world *feel* the effects of these cosmic frequency changes. And we've built entire systems as ways of interpreting and understanding these energies, systems that have been refined, used and adapted (and sometimes abused) over millennia. From Atlantis to Mesopotamia and Babylon, through ancient Greece to Los Angeles and Paris, the most dominant of those systems has been and continues to be astrology, a system of understanding ourselves based on star and planetary movements that has influenced and directed the ideas, decisions and beliefs of so many that have gone before.

Now, what if... what if other cultures had other ideas of what those energies meant? What if there was another way to interpret those star pathways? A way of myth and song, of victory and defeat, of life and death, a way that worked with the magic, mystery and medicine of the ancients and was really relevant for now?

What if you held that way in your hands?

Are you willing to explore ancient star paths to help navigate your future?

Then let us begin.

First, I'd like you to know me, my bias, what has led me here and why you would benefit from putting your trust and energy into me and all that I choose to share.

I'm a man, born and raised in Kent in England. I'm 6 feet 7 inches and big, I have a beard and I've spent a lot of the last 20 years dressed as a Viking (historical re-enactment has been my 'thing'). 'Vikingness', Nordic energetics and the northern wisdom tradition literally run through my blood and bones. My ancestry goes back to the Normans, and further back still to the Norwegian Vikings of Rollo the Walker.

While drinking my way through university, I discovered 'heathen paganism' and it felt good. I got to hang out in nature and talk with like-minded people, and this led me to the runes.

There was one focal event, and I shared this in my book *Runes Made Easy*, but it's important that I share it here too, in devotion and deep respect.

I was at a pagan camp in a field in the middle of an ancient forest. Most people had gone to sleep and the diehards were the only ones left around the fire.

This next bit is going to sound weird, but it's true.

I had a vision. A full-blown deity-standing-in-the-fire vision, telling me to go and learn about the northern traditions, to do better so I could serve better. I can't remember the exact words, but this was the gist. The deity had one eye and a spear. I was shaken to the core. Literally. From what I've been told, I stood there for half an hour staring at the fire, then silently turned around and went to my tent.

And because it's not an everyday occurrence to see who I now know was Odin, Nordic king of the gods, in the flames of a campfire, I went on to learn about the northern traditions in order to serve better.

Over the next decade and a half, I used the runes as I worked in a hospital Accident and Emergency Department, trained as a nurse and yoga teacher, learned Ayurveda, massage and NLP, and undertook psychological, psychotherapeutic and trauma training. I used the teachings and magic of the runes to co-create and construct my life and my reality. Marriage, moving house, changing careers – runes have been cast for guidance for them all, and I've allowed myself to be guided by them. They support me in trusting myself and trusting my personal power, and this is why I am passionate about sharing them as a supportive tool for others, because what I've learned is that so many of us have been stripped of our power, or given it away, either consciously or unconsciously. And yet we *all* have access to power, because it resides within, and we all knew how to wield power hundreds of years ago – the power to look into the mists of the future, the power to heal ourselves, the power to seek the correct help and guidance and make the right decisions.

This was why I wrote *Runes Made Easy*.

Except... there was more.

So much more.

The gods have spoken again, aware that we need the tools of the ancients so we can navigate our way through the choppy seas of the times we're currently in and co-create a better future.

The *Wyrd* has called me. The *Wyrd* is the place where all things are possible and all potential resides. As I explained in *Runes Made Easy*, it could be pictured as a shirt made up of millions of threads, each subtly influenced by those around it. Imagine what happens if you have a loose thread and you pull that thread – the threads around it become tight or loose, pucker up or flail away. This is what the *Wyrd* looks like. Every time we make a decision, that decision influences the threads around us.

In turn, the *Wyrd* can influence us – call us, as I was called. The celestial energies of the universe were seeking to be expressed. They showed up in how I worked and how I played – much to the annoyance of those around me, I'm sure!

Through this process, the thing that has become clear to me is that the language I previously used was that of a teacher, but I'm not a teacher, I'm a way-shower, a guide, a mentor. I'm not interested in teaching, I'm interested in showing the way we move and navigate through the universe. I'm here now, ready to show you how to navigate your way through life using runic astrology. Runic astrology takes the Vikings' runes, stories and myths and shows how they are expressed in the night sky, forming a cosmic map, a star path for us to follow.

Much of what we know about the ancient Nordic people has been lost, and what little remains has been through 1,000 years of propaganda, reinterpretation and nationalization. This leaves a void that has to be filled with knowledge and wisdom that come directly from the goddesses, gods, *Jotun* (giants) and *Svartalf* (dark elves or dwarves) of the Nordic pantheon, through trance, magic and dream.

This guide energy, mentor energy, is here for you in book form. To bring it to you, I've meditated for freaking ages. I've performed Viking rituals. I've gone under the cloak in power points across northern Europe to dream, travel and journey.

When a deer walks through woods or a person walks across grass, a pathway is formed. Broken branches, depressed grass, residual scent and sound all show where they have walked. And runic energies leave an imprint on the vibration of the universe as they move through it. They leave their marks, just as you can tell where your lover has slept on your pillow by their scent. And, like the deer and the lover, each rune has its own energetic imprint.

Out there in the cosmo-verse, I found the energetic trail of the runes. This trail has revealed how they resonate with the gigantic energetic powers of our solar system. How they interact and influence us on both an individual and a societal level. And how the censured and burned civilizations of old interpreted this energy.

You and I, using the tools, wisdom and power within this book, will be able to track the energetic influences of the runes across the cosmos – the Runic Star Paths.

Let me show you the way as you set off into the inky blackness of the sky. Let me point out to you the energy and passion available to you, the energetic vibrations that make the journey an experience of pleasure and bliss. Let me help you navigate these wild times in which we live. Let me show you the stars to navigate by.

Follow me, if you will, down the misty paths of the *Wyrd* to bring the energy and frequency you desire into your life. I will guide you through the rudiments of runic astrology, so that you can explore your own Runic Star Path. I'll share how to discover its main energetic resonances – your Sunna rune (Sun sign), Manni rune (Moon sign) and Jord (pronounced Yord) rune (rising sign) – and how to work with these resonances, and those of the gods in the skies, to co-create your life in the world.

Because we are part of the world, the universe, we are co-creators. And we co-create in relation to our experience of the world, the vibrational energy of the universe and how it affects us.

So, get ready to experience the energy and might of the ancient runes and walk your own Runic Star Path.

Astrology provides insights into your own energetic vibration – the way you do the things you do and why, and how you relate to others and interact with the world. It's also a way to forecast the future.

So what I'm calling for, what the northern tradition gods are calling for, is for you to immerse yourself in runic astrology, in all the Nordic myth and legend and the getting drunk in the mead hall that sits alongside the myth and legend, and, let's face it, the doom and tragedy of the Graeco-Roman stories. (Jeez, did those Greeks *love* a tragedy!)

Alongside is important. This is *not* a replacement for classic astrology, far from it. No one, least of all me, is saying, 'This way is right and that way is wrong.' Nope, this is purely an invitation, from me and the gods, to explore your terrain using your Runic Star Path.

I've been exploring mine for a number of years now, and I know runic astrology works. If you've had a Runic Star Path reading with me, you will know it works. But it's no good just a few of us knowing it. Of course, I'm always happy to offer Runic Star Path readings to those who ask, but I want runic astrology to be accessible and useful for *everyone* who hears the call of the ancients in the northern tradition.

So, are you ready now?

Then we shall begin.

OPENING RITUAL

Back in the ancient wooded fjords and burgs of the north, ritual and ceremony drove life, helping the people to build energetic resonance with the gods and the cosmos. These rituals were called *Blöts* (pronounced *bloats*, like '*boat*').

To activate your own connection with the powers of the universe, your Runic Star Path and the runes, I invite you perform your own *Blöt*.

Formerly, a *Blöt* was performed with a drink of mead or ale. In modern times, any drink of your choice will work. (In my experience, Thor likes chocolate milk.)

I carry out my *Blöts* around a fire. If you don't have space for a fire, a candle works fine. You'll also need a journal or notebook and a pen.

+ Light your candle and pour two drinks – one for yourself and one for the gods.

+ Take at least nine big slow breaths, counting in for seven and out for 11.

+ Feel your toes. Wiggle them.

+ Feel your legs. Bend and straighten them.

+ Feel your hips. Wiggle your butt.

+ Touch your belly, chest and arms with your hands.

+ Roll your neck this way and that way.

+ Wiggle your jaw and your tongue.

+ Rub your eyes.

+ Sip your drink.

+ In your journal, write down what comes to you when you hear the term 'Runic Star Paths'. What does that energy feel like to you?

- What colour is it?

- What texture is it?

- Does it have movement?

- Is it warm or cool?

- Is it hard or soft?

- Do any words, phrases or ideas come through?

- Make a note of anything and everything that you experience as a response. Even if it doesn't make any sense. Especially if it doesn't make any sense.

- Now sit in the energetics of your connection with the Runic Star Path concept. Give yourself a few minutes to see if anything else comes through.

- Then offer thanks to the gods and to the energetics of your own Runic Star Path. You can do this out loud with your voice or quietly in your mind. Both work.

- Stamp your feet. Clap your hands. Shout so loudly that the cat jumps.

- As your candle burns down, you can enjoy your drink. Or give it and the gods' one to a plant – something that will get nourishment from it.

This is an invitation,
from me and the gods, to
explore your terrain using
your Runic Star Path.

Chapter 1

What Is Runic Astrology?

In the far frozen north, on the harsh, sparse soil of the frozen fjords, power was etched into stone. This power was gifted from the gods and goddesses to the people to help them communicate, cast spells, divine the future and memorialize their lives.

It came in the form of runes.

RUNES

Runes are lines carved on rock, bone, metal or wood to convey meaning and energy. These ancient sigils – mystic symbols – are found carved onto primal rocks all over Scandinavia, and they extended their reach down to the Mediterranean, to France, Britain, and even, according to some, Canada.

The earliest runes, the Elder Furtharc, were used 1,700 years ago and were a series of 24 of these symbols, associated with sounds, like our alphabet. They were primarily an alphabet and were used to record the deeds of the brave and the noble, or document who owned a sword or a piece of land. They gave names, deeds and dates. There is even a runic calendar on a piece of bone marking 28 days – the length of an average menstrual cycle and/ or moon cycle.

The shapes and symbols of the runes started off relatively basic, expressing concepts drawn from their users' surroundings: beasts that stalked the lonely woodlands, thorns that ripped flesh, trees that grew. Community, family, seasons and elements were all held within the runes.

As time rolled on, the runes evolved. Different parts of Europe had slightly different versions, which grew through the people interacting with nature, the gods and the cosmic energies. In Scandinavia, the Elder Furtharc became the Younger Furtharc, which has more abstract ideas and fewer runes. The Saxons, Angles, Jutes and Northumbrians living in Britain had their own songs of the runes, and Northumbria even had extra runes. Denmark and the people around the Balkans had their own take on the runes too.

As the people who used the runes evolved, the magic of the runes followed suit. Different languages brought the need to make the runes fit the sounds the people were hearing and speaking.

Then, as Christianity spread, the ways of worship changed, the ways of making letters changed, and the mighty runestones began to grow moss.

Empires rose and fell, wars raged across the lands, and the energy of the runes lay dormant for hundreds of years, aside from in some isolated areas.

Now, as people are beginning once again to put effort and energy into working with the runes, their power is reawakening. Their energy is beginning to flow through a world that has moved on 800 years.

In that world, where so many of us are feeling stripped of or disconnected from our power, the runes allow us to reclaim it – to regain the power to look into the mists of the future, to support and heal ourselves, and to move in the right direction. They aren't fortune-tellers, but they are way-showers.

If you're new to the runes, I've made an easy-to-follow table that includes each rune and a brief interpretation:

Rune	Rune name	Pronunciation	Association
ᚠ	Fehu	Fee-huo	Wealth, abundance, reputation
ᚢ	Uruz	Urr-uhzz	Strength, power, stubbornness
ᚦ	Thurizaz	Thur-ee-sarz	Focus, cutting, sharpness
ᚨ	Ansuz	Ahn-sooz	Communication, magic, words, leadership
ᚱ	Raido	Ray-do	Adventure, curiosity, mobility
ᚲ	Kenaz	Ken-az	Self-belief, self-discovery, light in the darkness
ᚷ	Gebo	Gee-boh	Gifts, respect, mutual support
ᚹ	Wunjo	Wun-yo	Bliss, contentment, working towards those goals
ᚺ	Hagalaz	Ha-ga-laz	Change, renewal, surprise
ᚾ	Nauthiz	Naou-th-iz	Need, requirements, basics
ᛁ	Isaz	Eees-az	Glamour, distraction, smoothness

Rune	Rune name	Pronunciation	Association
⟩	Jera	Yer-ra	Harvest, fruitfulness, hard work
∫	Eihwaz	Yeehu-waz	Travelling through dimensions, changing states, holding energy
⊬	Peroth	Per-oth	Luck, sex, chance
⋎	Algiz	Al-geez	Boundaries, defence, standards
⟨	Sowolio	Sow-ol-io	Guidance, pathways, direction
↑	Tiwaz	Tee-waz or Tay-waz	Honour, leadership, doing the right thing
ß	Berkanan	Ber-karn-an	Regrowth, resilience, renewal
M	Ehwaz	Eh-waz	Trust, swiftness, friends
M	Mannaz	Man-ahz	Human spirit, human awesomeness, human resourcefulness
⌐	Laguz	Lah-gooz	Healing, water, washing away

Rune	Rune name	Pronunciation	Association
◇	Ingwaz	Ing-waz	Potential, heroic action, self-development
⛦	Othala	Oth-al-la	Home, castle, family
ᛟ	Dagaz	Dah-ghaz	Change, transition, new beginnings, the end of the old

Table 1: The Runes

HELLO, RUNES!

I'm so happy to share my interpretation of the runes and runic astrology, but it's really important that you build your own relationship with them and let them become alive and personal to you. Why not do the following:

• Draw each one in your journal.

• Add one or two words to each description. What energies do you feel are attracted to those runes?

Now that you know a little bit about the runes, we're going to explore how you can work with them each day to tune in to their magic, wisdom and guidance.

Runes are *meant* to be used. You can throw them on ceramics, paint them on things, draw them on your palm, and do some really good social media posts with them, if that's your thing. You can create magic spells by writing them on pieces of wood or bone or horn.

Rune Magic

Rune magic is a powerful way to really work with the forces of the universe to co-create the results that we want. This is where we *really* come into our power as rune workers. But how does it happen?

Well, runes are like magnets, or fuzzy felt. (Remember that? Just me... oh....) The point is, they stick to things. Magnets stick to ferrous metals, like steel and iron, so they are always drawn to those metals. Fuzzy felt sticks to other fuzzy felt. Lego pieces stick to other Lego pieces, and to feet at 3 a.m., if you're super tired and forgot to clear up after the kids. Ouch.

Each rune sticks to the energies that resonate, vibrate or pulse with its frequency. And how does that work?

Well, each rune is magical, but in the Nordic animist tradition *everything* holds magic, from the keyboard on your computer to the car I drive, to the tree in the field, the grass, the dirt, you, the cat, your clothes, and so on. Everything has magic, has energy, has spirit. Everything is a being. The way we treat other beings directly affects how they respond to us.

So, there's a connection between you and me and that thing. That rock? Connected to you. Did you plant that flower? Its energy is wrapped around yours. Do you have a dog? Guess whose energy is infused with yours?

All the energies in the universe are entangled. All have been spun into existence. Interacting with any of them, any thread, will have consequences. Grumpy today? The rock you kicked exposed a snail and caused it to get eaten by a crow, which caused the crow to be full of food, so it didn't eat the worm, and that allowed a baby sparrow to feed. All linked by energy weaving. In modern science, we call this 'the quantum field' or 'quantum entanglement'. In the ancient north, it was called the *Wyrd*. The idea has been around a while. Yogis knew everything was linked via energy, vibration, frequency, as did the Christian Church, the Islamic imams, the Druids and witches, and the *Völva* or *Spel-mann*, the magicians from the north. Essentially, this is how runic energy interacts with the universe – through quantum entanglement.

This is how rune magic works too, by attracting the energetic frequencies that will manifest your intent. When you or I make magic with the runes, we draw and magnetize threads of the *Wyrd* to us for a desired outcome.

Like the bind rune I wear on my necklace, for example. This is for protection and bliss. When I burned the rune into the bog oak, I called in certain energetics and frequencies to create the bind in the *Wyrd*. If I now want this rune to do other things, it won't work well. This is because it was constructed and created and infused and woven, in co-creation with the *Wyrd*, with a very clear intent.

So, rune magic requires both the power of intention and the activation of intention in time and space. Remember, though, that *everything* has spirit, and some things will resist being magic-ed. Others however, are more easily magnetized, like money for example.

Your adventure with the runes will also be helped by a basic understanding of the magical concepts within the Nordic energetic cosmos.

MAGICAL CONCEPTS OF THE NORTHERN TRADITION

The Wyrd

Fate, destiny, doom. Woven by the Norns, the three goddesses at the root of the world tree, the *Wyrd* is not as prescribed as Graeco-Roman fate, it's more of a guideline that we can influence, especially *with* the runes.

The *Wyrd* is always consensual. I'm not saying that bad stuff doesn't happen – the *Wyrd* can grab you so that you find yourself in a learning experience that you'd never have expected – but we do get to influence what happens.

Say you're getting on a bus. First of all, you choose to get on the bus that is going to where you want to go. Then you get to choose where you sit. If you choose to sit next to a weird guy with one eye and two ravens, you may have a different experience than if you choose to sit next to a body-builder with ginger hair. You also have to choose to get on the bus going the best way for you. Not going all over town and spending six hours in the back of beyond. Unless that's what you want. You do you boo.

Hamingja (Hai-ming-ya)

Luck or fortune. In the northern tradition, this can be recharged by being awesome. It's also more of a community gathered and gained energy than an individual one. When you're an effective part of your community and your community supports you, your luck increases. Do good, get good. There is more on this later.

Yggdrasil (Yig-dra-sil)

The cosmos is connected by a tree, the world tree, a giant ash called Yggdrasil. At its foot, the Norns weave the *Wyrd*.

Norns

I mentioned these earlier, and they are quite the crux of belief and magic in the northern tradition. The Norns are three goddesses – Urðr (Fate), Verðandi (Now) and Skuld (What Will Happen) – who sit at the foot of the world tree and spin the very fabric of the universe into reality. Just knowing they are around, weaving the threads of universal energy into the complex quilt that is life, the universe and everything, is important.

Völva and Spel-Mann (Vohl-va and Spell-man)

These were the magic users, the wise people, those who accessed the deep and connective energies back in the ancient north. A *Völva*, witch, tended to be female, a *Spel-Mann* male. *Ergi* (*Err-ghe*) were those between genders, those in modern language we'd call 'trans' or 'non-binary'. The ancient Nordic people realized the *Ergi* could connect with different energies in the universe.

Asir

These are the gods and goddesses of the northern pantheon, who normally live in Asgard, a beautiful world of green valleys and towering walls at the top of the world tree, and are quite interested in people.

Vanir

Another tribe of gods, but more interested in farming and fertility than in people.

Jotun (Yo-tun)

Primitive tribal gods of the elemental and primal energies, often called giants. The Saxons called them *Etin*. These gods are interested in the energies that existed before humankind started farming. They don't really care about humans, and unless they respect you, they can be downright hostile.

Now, with the ideas, concepts and myths built into runic astrology starting to resonate in your energy, your aura, let us begin to journey into the cosmos of the runes.

ASTROLOGY

Astrology is looking for patterns in the stars and planets. It's mythology in the skies, stories and magic told through astral movements. It's a cosmic guidance system from ancient Greece, Babylon, Persia and Mesopotamia that has evolved over thousands of years, drawing on people's experience of life and making correspondences with how events and people show up in the world.

Over the generations, through different cultures and epochs, different pantheons of deities and different rulers and ideologies, it has been refined and defined, and now we find ourselves with a very well-honed system for interpreting the cosmic influences on our experience of the world. From weekly magazines with 'star signs' on the back pages, to daily papers with 'horoscopes', to broadsheets with full-page astrology segments, there's a lot of astrological guidance out there. Hundreds of books are written every year to teach us astrology, and tens of thousands of people provide astrological readings and other services around the globe. What we have now is massive collective power to understand the subtle influences of the cosmos on our experience.

How I see astrology is like this. We have the sun that provides life to our little blue ball in the darkness. The sun transmits energy, and that energy isn't consistently the same – there are different sunspots, solar flares, vibrations, and resonances at work. So from day to day, minute to minute, we get hit by a unique combination of solar rays. Those rays make our food grow, and we eat the food, so we get to consume and experience the energy of the sun in many different ways.

Another science thing is that *everything* has a gravitational pull. Something big like a planet or star has a bigger pull than something little like a kitten, me, or a moon.

But, and this is important, even those little gravitational pulls change how energy moves. So, the energy hitting us from the sun goes through the filter of the gravitational energy of the other planets and asteroids in the solar system, and –

this is the fun bit – it is also impacted by the constellations that form our astrological zodiac.

The Zodiac

The zodiac is a band of sky with 12 different constellations in it, all named after Greek myth, and all with dates assigned to them, which are static from year to year:

Aries	♈	21 March – 19 April
Taurus	♉	20 April – 20 May
Gemini	♊	21 May – 20 June
Cancer	♋	21 June – 22 July
Leo	♌	23 July – 22 August
Virgo	♍	23 August – 22 September
Libra	♎	23 September – 22 October
Scorpio	♏	23 October – 21 November
Sagittarius	♐	22 November – 21 December
Capricorn	♑	22 December – 19 January
Aquarius	♒	20 January – 18 February
Pisces	♓	19 February – 20 March

Table 2: The Zodiac

These have an energetic cycle, starting in Aries and finishing in Pisces, and getting 'wiser' and more developed as it progresses. Think of Aries energy as 16-year-old you and Pisces energy as 65-year-old you.

Everyone, according to this system, has a zodiac sign, according to their date of birth. I'm a Libra and my wife is a Scorpio, as is King Charles III. My editor is a Taurus.

I'm not going to explain astrology in full, as there are many different versions and ways of understanding it. I'm guessing that as you're here you might know a little about it already, and I'll share the parts that you'll need in order to activate your Runic Star Path. I do think that knowing what energies affected you as the first solar and cosmic rays hit your infant skin is important, as those codes went deep into your body, mind and aura. These are what we'll access when working with your Runic Star Path.

To be honest, though, classical astrology is a discipline that I've often found hard to grasp, even though I've a good knowledge of classical myth, and it wasn't until I met my wife that I was able to understand it more fully.

Lisa, my radiant wife, delves into the feminine stories of the stars and planets. She comes from a line of women who are what's called in the Traveller tradition *Sky Readers*, which means they care little for the 'mathematics' of astrology and instead feel the energetics of the stars and planets through their body. It was the realisation of 'Wait, there's more than one way to do this?' that made it easier for me to start exploring astrology on my own terms.

Naturally enough, I asked the gods of the northern tradition for their support.

'What is the navigation tool we need for now? Is it astrology? Is there a way we can work with the runes *and* astrology to navigate these current times and co-create our future?'

Their response? Well, it's what you have here in your hands. It's been collaborative and channelled with the gods. It's runic astrology.

RUNIC ASTROLOGY

Runic astrology is a guide to the cosmos through the lens of the northern tradition. It fits completely into the mechanics of classical astrology, but the zodiac of the runes adds different stories, myths and vibrations to the astrology we've known before. The heroic nature of northern spirituality brings a unique cosmological view of the universe.

What is important to note is that runic astrology could not exist in its current form without classical astrology and astronomy. Thousands of years of study of the celestial energies and planetary bodies have led us to where we are now, and there is zero point in reinventing the wheel and making things complex, so the maths and science have been carried over. Runic astrology is simply another way of looking at the energies that spin from the galactic centre. It's applying the myths, mysteries and majesty of the ancient Nordic tribes to the dots of light in the sky above that influence our lives, and using them, *collaborating* with them, to navigate and co-create our lives.

Much as CT scans see bones and soft tissue one way and MRI scans see them another, and our eyes see them another, and ultrasound yet another, classical astrology and runic astrology see the same world though different lenses. Quite literally, the iron-grey mountains, cloud-covered sky and inky black sea of the north are far from the burning sky and azure sea of the Mediterranean. The context and references are different.

Runic astrology can actually be considered to give a more detailed view, because it has twice as many data points. So we can get a little more precise about the energies that are affecting and influencing us.

Also, classical astrology is a system that is often prescriptive and can sometimes use fear-based language, along the lines of 'If you don't do this, that will happen.' What runic astrology tries to do is reframe this into a more open system that is designed to help you grow, develop and become more powerful in yourself.

What's important to remember is that different lenses provide different views and insights. More insights provide more wisdom, and more wisdom leads to better decisions.

I love looking at the world through many different lenses.

I want to help you to see life slightly differently too, and the lens of runic astrology is one that allows you to conjure up and feel empowered to work with the cosmic vibrations of the universe to navigate your Runic Star Path through life.

So, where to begin?

Let's Start at the Beginning...

Back in the day, we didn't mark calendar years, but we knew that spring followed winter, summer followed spring, autumn followed summer and winter followed autumn. That was as accurate as life got, time-wise. Farmers knew when to sow and they knew when to reap.

As culture developed, we added more structure to our experience of the year.

The earliest calendar in the north was carved on a bone comb. I mentioned it earlier. It marked a 28-day cycle. This calendar grew into a formalized way of counting moons, 13 a year.

When kings, armies and taxes came, more formulation was required. There were many different calendars in the ancient world. The old Roman calendar had 304 days divided into 10 months, starting with March, with the remaining days unaccounted for in the winter. Then January and February were brought into the count, and later still some ego got involved, and Julius Caesar and Augustus added their names to the calendar and made further revisions.

Time moved on and the runic calendar was devised, starting when the days were at their longest, with the most light in the sky.

And then came 1582, and the Julian calendar was reorganized by Pope Gregory to form the Gregorian calendar. The ins and outs of this aren't that important, but from a runic astrology perspective, one date moved. At first, midsummer was around 10 July, but when Pope Gregory moved stuff around, actual midsummer fell on 21 June. This moved the start month of the runic calendar.

While there can be some variance in dates, I've formalized the runic calendar to start on 21 June, which is usually the summer solstice.

And now we know where to begin, let's look ahead. What are we going to explore on our journey through runic astrology?

✦ The birth chart or natal chart – this shows the cosmic pattern at the time of our birth (though a birth chart can be drawn up for other things, too, such as nation states) and how this influences us.

+ Nornir runes – how to access our luck and superpowers.

+ The runic elements and how the runes form relationships. And how we can use this to work out who to date/work with/choose a puppy with.

+ The planets as gods – their energies and interests. How they interact with us and their influence.

+ Wandering gods – what it means when the gods get bored of their throne and 'go retrograde' or wander around.

+ The world tree – how it throws shade (not like that) and how that energy influences our energy.

+ And, most importantly, the runic zodiac. This is a huge one, so we will concentrate on the Sunna (Sun), Manni (Moon) and Jord (Earth/rising) runes, the three main energies in runic astrology, and their importance for our Runic Star Path.

So, let's step onto that path. What are Runic Star Paths and where do they lead?

Runic astrology provides
the cognitive constructs
for our brain to
understand the unseen
energies of the cosmos.

Chapter 2

Runic Star Paths

R unic Star Paths are the routes of the stars and planets that
move around the cosmos. Remember the ancients did *not*
see a difference between the dot in the sky that is the planet
Jupiter and the dot that is the Andromeda galaxy. They saw
stars. Therefore, Runic Star Paths. 'Runic' because in runic
astrology, the celestial bodies are symbolized by runes.

These paths can be plotted on a map, showing the energies,
cosmic vibrations and frequencies that interact with us. Your
own Runic Star Path explores the movements of the cosmos
in relation to your own lived experience and supports
you in feeling into those energetics, navigating them and
co-creating with them.

LENSES OF MAGICAL ENERGY

You remember that planets have a gravitational pull? Well, one of the things this does is to distort how energy moves through it.

Have you ever watched someone in a swimming pool? They look weird, as if their body is tiny and their head is normal size. The gravitational pull of the planets does this to the cosmic energies.

Another way of looking at this is as a lens. I've got some blue light blocking glasses that I put on at night to stop my brain being fried. The lenses of these glasses stop blue light from hitting my brain. And light is a form of energy.

So, what happens when energy flows past a planet is that certain frequencies, certain vibrations, get distorted or blocked.

Each planet has a lens effect of its own, blocking energies it doesn't like and allowing and even amplifying energies it does. So, when we look through the lens of a planet's influence, we see the world how that celestial energy sees it.

The frequencies of these energies are translated by our brain. Now, I'm going to go off on a bit of a tangent right now. It's worth it.

Back in the 1500s, when Europeans were sailing all over the world to trade, the Indigenous peoples of many other lands found this to be a completely new experience.

The European sailors couldn't understand why the Indigenous peoples didn't respond to the arrival of their big ships, but when they put the tenders out, the natives sent dug-out canoes.

The new experience was the thing. We tell stories to help ourselves cope with the unknown. What if there were no stories about sailing ships in your culture's history? Would you have the mental ability to see them? Or would your brain simply shut off and say, 'Nope, not dealing'?

We know that the brain says 'no' in these circumstances.

Runic astrology provides the cognitive constructs for our brain to understand the unseen, or to be more accurate the previously unseen, energies of the cosmos. As you learn how the vibrations that come from the stars and planets work together, you'll see where the runes show up with this energy.

The runes are our MRI scanner for cosmic energies, allowing us to grasp the messages, stories and insights that come from the stars.

Because everything on this planet is made from and fuelled by star energy, everything has a runic resonance. So, the paths of the stars influence how grass grows, how cows moo and how llamas... do whatever llamas do. What do llamas do? (Spit, I believe....)

What I'd like you to be able to do, to feel into, when you finish this book is to find your birth runes and those of your friends and family. And cat, dog, goldfish, etc. Then, when you know what influences are in your life, you can navigate your way forward. You can identify a good day for, say, finding love. Or telling a story.

EVOLVING MYTHS

Aettir (Et-tear), families and communities, were big parts of the ancient Nordic mindset, with huge amounts of interdependence between people. This interdependence, and the need to tell stories about everything (our Nordic ancestors loved a story), brings the concept of *Aettir* into the runic universe. The runes themselves are broken up into three families of eight runes.

The runic *Aettir* tell the story of life from the basics of survival to the growth of a person and a species. This isn't a story like that of the Tarot, which has a very clear and well-defined narrative, it's much more about the evolution of concepts:

+ The first *Aett* represents the individual, starting with resources (Fehu) and ending with joy (Wunjo).

+ The second *Aett* is how the individual is tested, weathers the storm and can grow and develop, starting with change (Hagalaz) and ending with the sun (Sowolio).

+ The third and final *Aett* tells the story of how the individual becomes part of society, starting with duty and honour

(Tiwaz) and ending with initiation and passing through the doorway to the beyond (Dagaz).

In runic astrology, the runes progress from a land of peace, with Fehu and Uruz, slowly building more strife and learning as they move through the runic cosmo-verse until, by Wunjo, it's all nice, with gifts, adventures and bliss. Then the tone changes to one of strife, with hail, hunger and fire, then mellows with lessons learned, luck, edges and pathways, before moving into honour, resilience, companionship and family.

So the runes tell a very basic story of initiation, of becoming a meaningful part of the community through the trials of life and becoming more powerful, before transitioning at the end back to the beginning.

The energies follow the seasons through the runic calendar of the year, with Hagalaz, Nauthiz and Isaz, hail, lack and ice, coming in the darkest parts of the year, when life is hardest. When it's coldest, when resources are low, luck plays a part, with Peroth, as do strong boundaries, with Algiz. Then life gets easier if you trust yourself and the process as the seasons change and the year moves on.

The runes are a map to victory throughout the year. If you follow it, you'll have victory in your life.

*The energies that arrive
in our bodies and in our
souls at the moment of
our birth are mapped in
our Runic Star Paths.*

Chapter 3

The Birth Chart

The birth chart, or natal chart, of classical astrology, the Runic Star Path of runic astrology, is one of our pivotal tools. It tells us where the planets, asteroids and constellations were when we popped out of our momma — the energetic reverberation that flowed through us at the moment of our birth. It reveals the pattern and path laid out for us by the Norns.

THE NORNS

The Norns, as you now know, are three powerful goddesses whose role is to create the fates of all things. They spin the threads of fate on a celestial spinning wheel, using the very stuff of the universe to create the stories and complex experiences of life.

✦ Urðr (Fate) takes the stuff of the universe, the atoms, energy and vibration of creation, and feeds it to her sister Verðandi (Now).

✦ Verðandi (The Happening) takes it and spins it into threads, creating what we can become.

✦ Skuld (What Will Happen) takes the strands and uses them to create the infinitely complex paths of vibration and frequency that all life follows.

So, these goddesses create patterns, the web, that we live our life on, in and through.

ENERGETICS

But, and this is an important but, we – you and I, the cat, the planet, the gods and goddesses, the spider plant – get to choose how we interact with that energy. We aren't pawns in some giant game of chess. We are autonomous and get to choose to pick up the threads of life or not. Sometimes that choice is hard, but we do get it.

And, though we are really quite small on the scale of the universe, we have big potential. Kind of like a toddler on a long-distance flight, we are small but the impact we can have is huge. We can influence the universe around us. And in turn be influenced (unlike the in-flight toddler).

How does it work? We have a massively complex body full of nerves and neurons, cells, bones and all the squishy bits in the middle, a body that acts as an antenna for the cosmic frequencies that can affect us. Like tuning a radio, we can pick up different cosmic energies if we act in different ways. We become *magnetic* to them, and *this* is where the power lies....

When we are born, the Norns give us an energetic resonance, a frequency that pulls certain energy to us. This energy is a double-edged sword that can limit as well as enliven. Because life isn't that simple. But by mapping the energies of the cosmos at that moment, we can see how our cells and neurons were influenced by the world outside the protective film of the womb, and so understand our inherent strengths and weaknesses.

This is looking at cosmic energy from an epigenetics standpoint – modification of gene expression. According to epigenetics, certain genes in our DNA are turned on or off in response to environmental factors. It's been suggested that trauma can trigger or repress genes, even intergenerationally. So it's not much of a jump to consider that the cosmic rays that we experience every day can turn on and turn off DNA codes in our body when we are born. This is what our birth chart shows: the energies that affect our DNA when we are born.

By knowing which energies were present, we can understand our personality traits, propensity to environmental factors, strengths, weaknesses and preferences.

So the birth chart is like a guidebook to the energetic body. Much like a mechanic will have a service manual for your car, your birth chart is the service manual for your life.

LOOKING AT YOUR BIRTH CHART

The birth chart is the basic chart that most, if not all, astrology software on the internet or in app form will give you. You don't need to pay for it. Literally search on the internet for 'birth chart' or 'natal chart' and you should have lots of free options.

Sooo... If you've not already done that, go do it.

Some things you need to make sure your chart has are the degrees which each of the planets, signs and asteroids are in.

Access your birth chart and print it out. Fold it in half and stick it in the cover of your journal, or in this book. Having it on paper means you can access it wherever and draw all over it.

CONNECTING WITH YOUR BIRTH CHART

Open up your chart. If you're using a digital chart, bring it up on your phone or tablet.

I put music on for this and you may like to do the same. I choose Wardruna (current favourite, 'Lyfjaberg').

Now, with the intent of connecting with, activating and receiving from your chart, place your hand on the chart.

Place your other hand on the centre of your chest, over your sternum and heart. Feel your breath lift that hand.

Breathe for a couple of minutes, connecting to the energies that are flowing to you from the cosmos, through your Runic Star Path, your birth chart.

When you feel you have finished, thank the energies and grab some chocolate or some other treat.

Stamp your feet, eat the chocolate and get ready for the energy to come. What sort of energy? Well, cosmic energy can feel like a sugar rush. Depending on how much chocolate you've just snaffled.

Now you have connected with the energies of the cosmos that the Norns have woven into your soul's energetic tapestry. The runes that are woven into this tapestry are known as your *glóa stigr* (*Glow-a St-eye-g*) or Glowing Path Makers.

Sounds good, right? *Glowing Path Makers*. Let's look at three of the most influential.

Your Wyrd is woven by the
Norns – the threads held
in your Runic Star Path.

Chapter 4

The Sunna, Manni and Jord Runes

We're going to start simple here, by looking at the main energetic influences on your DNA, namely the goddess Sunna (the Sun), the god Manni (the Moon), and the goddess Jord (the Earth/your rising sign), and I'm going to tell you how to work out what yours are.

So, let's get looking through the pile of papers that your birth chart is in, so you've got it to hand. If you're super organized, unlike me, you may even have folded it up and used it as a bookmark. Get it out, as we are going to be using it in a minute.

SUNNA (THE SUN)

Let's start with the biggest energy pull in the solar system: the sun, Sunna. (The sun is feminine in the Nordic pantheon, as it brings life to the frozen north, whereas in Mediterranean or African paganism the sun tends to be male, as there it can burn or kill.) She puts out loads of energy too, so you get a double whammy. This is why the Sunna rune, or Sun sign, is so important.

Sunna likes to put people on the right path, show the way and help things happen. She provides energy, guidance and light.

What kind of guidance does Sunna give you? What sort of energy does she attract?

I'm going to assume that you've got your birth chart. Look for the circle with a dot in the middle.

Make a note of the zodiac sign it is in – this is your Sun sign – and the degree. For example, Sun is at 24° of Libra.

We'll look at how to translate this into a rune in a moment.

MANNI (THE MOON)

Then find the sign with the symbol of a crescent moon and again note down the degree.

My Moon is at 22° of Virgo.

JORD (EARTH/RISING)

Now look at what would be about 9 o'clock if your chart were a clock. There you'll see a line, like a horizon. Again, note down the sign this is in. This is your rising sign, the sign rising up above the horizon when you were born. Again, note down the sign and the degree.

My rising sign is 14° of Libra.

SIGNS AND RUNES

So, you've got three data points. I know you love data points. And you know what I keep saying about data points? The more you have, the more accurate you can be.

Your Sunna Rune

To find your Sunna rune, the simplest way is to check the following table. You'll see that while each zodiac sign has about 30 days assigned to it, in runic astrology each rune has about 15 days. This makes the energy association of runic astrology that much more accurate than classical astrology.

Birth rune	Date start (at midday)	Date end (at midday)
Fehu	21 June	7 July
Uruz	7 July	23 July
Thurizaz	23 July	7 August
Ansuz	7 August	23 August
Raido	23 August	8 September
Kenaz	8 September	23 September
Gebo	23 September	8 October
Wunjo	8 October	23 October
Hagalaz	23 October	7 November
Nauthiz	7 November	22 November
Isaz	22 November	7 December
Jera	7 December	22 December
Eihwaz	22 December	6 January
Peroth	6 January	20 January
Algiz	20 January	4 February
Sowolio	4 February	19 February
Tiwaz	19 February	5 March
Berkanan	5 March	20 March
Ehwaz	20 March	4 April
Mannaz	4 April	19 April
Laguz	19 April	5 May
Ingwaz	5 May	20 May
Othala	20 May	5 June
Dagaz	5 June	21 June

Table 3: Birth Rune Dates

Your Manni and Jord Runes

Still got your Post-its with the degrees on? Awesome. Check out the table below and you'll find your Manni rune and Jord rune (and your Sunna rune again, if you wish).

Fehu	0 – 15 degrees Cancer
Uruz	16 – 30 degrees Cancer
Thurizaz	0 – 15 degrees Leo
Ansuz	16 – 30 degrees Leo
Raido	0 – 15 degrees Virgo
Kenaz	16 – 30 degrees Virgo
Gebo	0 – 15 degrees Libra
Wunjo	16 – 30 degrees Libra
Hagalaz	0 – 15 degrees Scorpio
Nauthiz	16 – 30 degrees Scorpio
Isaz	0 – 15 degrees Sagittarius
Jera	16 – 30 degrees Sagittarius
Eihwaz	0 – 15 degrees Capricorn
Peroth	16 – 30 degrees Capricorn
Algiz	0 – 15 degrees Aquarius
Sowolio	16 – 30 degrees Aquarius
Tiwaz	0 – 15 degrees Pisces
Berkanan	16 – 30 degrees Pisces
Ehwaz	0 – 15 degrees Aries
Mannaz	16 – 30 degrees Aries
Laguz	0 – 15 degrees Taurus
Ingwaz	16 – 30 degrees Taurus
Othala	0 – 15 degrees Gemini
Dagaz	16 – 30 degrees Gemini

Table 4: Degrees of the Runes in the Zodiac

If your degree is 15 point something, read it as 16.

Boom! You have your Runic Star Path.

Thank you. Book over. Or this chapter at least.

Ready for the next bit? Want to know what it all means?

Know yourself better
through the astrological
and cosmological vibration
of your Runic Star Path.

Chapter 5

Finding Your Runic Resonance

ow you know your three main runic energies, you can begin to understand your Runic Star Path. Prepare to see the magic that is happening around you – the energy that is being magnetized into your life, ready for you to work with.

And get your Post-its and highlighter ready, for this is one of the reference bits of the book. Don't get overwhelmed, just look up the wisdom that's applicable to you.

SUNNA RUNE – YOUR SOUL PURPOSE

Sunna is a pathway and direction energy, and a Sunna rune is a rune that illuminates your guiding path. Like a spiritual streetlamp!

Your Sunna rune shows your soul purpose and I advise you to use it as a guide for decision-making. If you act with its energy in mind, you won't go far wrong.

Let's look at how your Sunna rune energy guides you through life.

Fehu

With Fehu as your Sunna rune, your guiding light leads you to bring abundance and fertility to yourself and those around you. Fehu is the rune of Frey, the fertility god, and provided you live your life in ways that increase wealth, abundance and fertility, you will have no problem feeling fulfilled.

Your soul will also be happy when you are building up your reputation. The more people have your name on their lips (either your real name or an assumed name, as long as it's yours), the greater the flow of energy into your life. Resources will flow to you, and in turn those resources will bring growth to your reputation and standing in your community.

When you use your ability to manifest resources, abundance, fertility and/or reputation, you'll find that those around you will quite literally vibrate with your excess. You ensure that those who work for you or with you have what they need, and they in turn ensure that you have what you need.

Uruz

Your Sunna rune is attracted to the raw, wild power of Uruz, the aurochs, which can be expressed either physically or energetically, or indeed both. A wild man o' the mountains-type approach, or being in wild places, or both, will fill you with power.

Be warned, though, that constraints that don't meet with your ethics mean nothing to you, so you are likely to quickly trample over them or ignore them entirely, and others may not feel the same way. To avoid conflict, learn the skills that will help you live by *your* rules without antagonizing others.

You are driven by the power to be wild and untamed in thought, word and deed, so putting yourself in places where your wildness will serve you will lead to victory and contentment. Power, stubbornness and strength will see you through, but you choose when to apply them. Remember, 'to a hammer, everything looks like a nail'. But when necessary, go forth and bash things out of your way!

Thurizaz

Thurizaz is a rune of focus and direct action. This energy is that of a magnifying glass held under the midday sun, or the prick of a thorn, or the focus of a laser pointer. This is where you can find your power and pathway.

When you act, choose to focus on one thing and put your not inconsiderable power into it. This way, your energy isn't being bled away into areas where it's under-utilized. For you, success, victory and contentment come from not deviating from your focus.

You don't want to be having to change direction a long way down the path, so stop every now and then to check the lie of the land. In fact, short sharp bursts of action are probably your friends – going forward with power and grace, but stopping before you get exhausted and blunt.

Your wit, humour and world-view may well be sharp and cutting, like the claw of a cat, or a thorn in a bush. But they're always to the point!

Ansuz

 Ansuz is the rune of the voice, words and leadership, and as such is the rune of Odin (Mercury). The Runic Star Path it sets out is one of communication, leadership and inspiration. With Ansuz as your Sunna rune, you'll find this energy flowing to you.

Look to where your voice can get you into – and out of – situations that you are required to be in. Remember words are magic, yours especially. Words are power, and using the right words will ease your path through life.

With power flowing in the direction of leadership and creativity, look to where you can be in charge, be seen or otherwise be important thanks to your creativity and voice. This is where huge power lies for you.

When life gets hard, remember that your path is smoothed with words and magic. Use your voice, use your magic. Your biggest allies will come if you form your words in ways they can grasp and resonate with.

Raido

Wanderlust – this is the radiant energy that flows through your Sunna rune. Setting out on an adventure is powerful magic for you. Be it for healing or joy, or both!

Being constantly curious and ready to find out what's on the other side of the mountain is the way that you'll find bliss and contentment in life. Do you always want to travel? Or do you want to find out how this molecule bonds with that one? Or do you want to explore how to create amazing art to inspire others? Whatever your preferred form of exploration, you have the power and the drive to see what's 'over there'.

Don't be afraid to bring others along for the journey, as your innate adventurous spirit will enthuse them. If they do have a tantrum at any time, they can just sit on a bench while you go and look at that amazing thing over there.

Trust your adventurous spirit. It will never lead you wrong.

Kenaz

 With Kenaz flowing through Sunna's energy, you are doubly blessed with light energy to use as you see fit. Are you a 'lightworker', by any chance?

Finding what is hidden in the darkness may be a superpower of yours. Hidden things probably drive you potty. Kenaz wants to shine light everywhere, and it's this energy that will propel you forward. Forward with insatiable curiosity....

This runic resonance is your pathway to victory and heroic achievements. Consider where you can bring enlightenment to situations. Where you can chase away ignorance and darkness from yourself and from others. Where you can shed light on the hidden or disguised things that others ignore. This is your power. Don't be afraid to use it.

You may find that people are drawn to you when the unknown or confusing arise. This is also part of your heroic path, as you are a beacon of light and safety in the darkness.

Gebo

Gebo and Sunna are a combination that enhances your innate talents. Your ability to bring life, light and love to the environment around you is of huge importance and can have far-reaching effects.

This runic energy calls you to strive for self-expression in any way that feels good to you. Clothes, jobs, pastimes, lovers – anything that helps you express your energy will help you fulfil your soul purpose.

The celestial combination of Gebo and Sunna also indicates a personality that is driven to seek out the messages, gifts and secrets of the esoteric. Delving into the *Wyrd* and wonderful ways of the cosmos will bring you victory and fulfilment.

This curiosity, this drive to seek out obscure facts and remarkable things, will in turn set your innate talents pulsing for more – more exploration, more adventures, more looking, feeling and being awesome.

To utilize this energy in your cells and molecules, ensure that you are feeling and looking as you would like. This will allow your power to radiate out fully.

Wunjo

As the nights get longer and the animals and resources are brought in, your Wunjo energy shines through. Your ability, both energetically and practically, to make sure that everyone's needs are met will stand you in good stead in the communities in which you find yourself.

Your frequency drives you to seek contentment and do the work to get it. This makes you the ideal person to have around when things get stressful or unsettled. Finding, or building, bridges between people and making sure needs are met are your superpowers. So, you may be drawn to caring roles, or leadership ones. Wunjo isn't all fluffy blanket hugs, it's also the discipline that ensures that wood is chopped and water carried. And everything else is done to make sure that needs are met.

Your energy is very communal. This shows itself in how you lead and how you follow. And you want to be *comfortable*. If the basic tasks aren't done properly, it will probably drive you mad.

Hagalaz

At first glance, a soul purpose of 'Crush everything and everyone around me' may not be the most inspiring destiny. Or, with a Hagalaz Sunna rune, maybe it is.

This is taking Hagalaz at a very, very surface level, however. On a deeper one, Hagalaz is the ability to take what has gone before and use its death as fuel. Where others despair, you see opportunity. You see a situation, let it be resolved and then empower yourself through the learnings, adventures and experiences you receive as a result.

So, trust yourself in challenging situations, as your instincts will aid you in fuelling yourself and becoming even more powerful than you can possibly imagine.

Also, look to the experiences in life that fill you up, that make your heart sing and your soul yearn. These experiences, too, will fuel you and your exploration of life. And with Hagalaz energy, *you* happen to situations. Not the other way around.

Nauthiz

Your Sunna energy shines through the lens of Nauthiz, the rune of need. At first glance, this is a rune of suffering and pain. But while that energy is there, this rune brings a resolute power. It's not all doom and gloom, trust me.

The guiding light of Sunna shining through the energy of need brings you the tendency to be guided by your will. Your focus and your devotion to your ideas bring you the ability to create and be artistic.

Truth, honesty, loyalty and independence are guiding factors in your life, and your optimism is rooted in them. If someone hides the truth or tries to be dishonest, it is likely to cause you confusion and pain. They may well become dead to you.

Acting in ways that build loyalty and trust in yourself and others will always help you create and achieve your goals and bring you victory.

Isaz

Isaz is a twofold rune, with both glamour and distraction in place. Like a woolly mammoth in a glacier. And, like a glacier, Isaz moves slowly but inevitably.

With Isaz as your Sunna rune, look to find your life purpose in the unstoppable movement towards a goal. Or the distraction and glamour of glittering ice sculptures. You get to choose, as you are epic. Choose to crush everything in front of you with your unstoppable will. Or, if the mood takes you, dazzle all around you with glamour and misdirection like a hall of mirrors.

This dual path can lead you to acquire an interesting skill-set of being steady and reliable and getting everything done, while appearing bright and shiny and too good to be true.

Remember, though, that ice doesn't like heat, and pressure makes heat. Keep yourself cool and don't let others take advantage of your work ethic. Just let them be distracted by the shiny things, while you get stuff done. Remember, you cannot be stopped.

Jera

Your soul purpose is wrapped around the rune of Jera, the rune of harvest and rewards. Everyone likes rewards, so why is this special for you?

Well, Jera energy hinges on the work being done to get the best harvest. Your ability to make sure that the right things are done at the right time for the required result is a manifestation of this energy.

You, awesome one, are able to bring the energy of manifestation into the real world with more ease than others. Your manifestation ability is that of the farmer growing a crop. They know exactly what they will get if they follow their plan. This is how your energy flows – it's methodical, organized and focused. It will make sure all the steps are completed, even though you may not think about this consciously, or even realize it.

If your harvest hasn't yet come, check out where you have given up power to others and taken your energy away from your process.

Eihwaz

Your soul purpose is very wrapped up in your ability to manage. Manage energy, not pushing papers in an office kind of manage. Well... maybe, if that's your jam. But mainly managing energy so it flows consistently for all those you care about. Even if that's just you and the cat.

Essentially, Eihwaz is the rune of energy control. So, storing and using energy is part of your soul purpose, be it practically with electrics or fire, or in more esoteric ways like energy healing or things of an oracular nature. Or in interactions with people, getting the best from a team, or friend, or situation.

You get to choose the energy you store. Storing negative energy would be an 'interesting' experience, kind of like putting rotten leftovers in the fridge, whereas storing positive energy will provide a very different experience. This ability to store energy makes it easy for you to be included in parties, rituals or other energetic experiences, as you bring the magic naturally.

Peroth

Peroth is a two-dimensional rune, the first dimension being luck. In the time of the Vikings, luck was called *Hamingja*. It was earned by hard work. The more you contributed to the collective, the luckier you would be. This was true for everyone. You, though, with a Peroth Sunna rune, have this on steroids. Luck may well find its way into your life, maybe not on a lottery-win level, but on an everyday level. The universe has your back. Follow the unexpected, as this has great potential for you.

The other aspect of Peroth is sex, so follow your sexual energy too, as this will lead to passion and imagination not just between the sheets, but in every corner of your life.

Sexual energy is also the energy of potential and joy – the potential of conception, the joy of that act, the potential creative energy contained within.

Combined, these two energies bring a powerful vibration to your life, one that will drive you to be inventive and resilient. And lucky.

Algiz

With Algiz as your Sunna tune, you will have strong and powerful boundaries and standards, as Algiz brings you a strong sense of edges, and when to cross them and when to hold them.

When you choose to let boundaries be crossed, either by you or by others, you are empowered. This is Algiz energy. When they are crossed inadvertently, through your apathy or inattention, your energy is sapped. When you let people walk over you or take advantage, because of social conditioning or a need to be a 'good' person, your energy will be depleted, leaving you to get sick.

When you choose to be strong in your standards and boundaries, however, Algiz will bring you safety and power. And in turn your Algiz energy will spread to your kith and kin. Their boundaries will be stronger because of you. This is how you manifest your heroic destiny.

Sowolio

With Sowolio, rune of the sun, navigation and guidance, as your Sunna rune, your Runic Star Path is that of the way-shower. When you stand up, people follow. You have the ability to lead by inspiration or, like the sun in the desert, to burn up those around you. Your call.

You can also choose to quietly motivate and encourage as a teacher or mentor, or to stand at the front of the line as you stride forth into the uncharted jungle. Any way you choose to motivate, lead or show the way will work.

Being a way-shower can lead you into coaching, therapy, leadership and ownership. A manager you are not – petty BS isn't going to cut it with you – you are about getting on the right path and following it. And not just your own right path, but the path that is right for those you are leading. Showing people the way is your heroic purpose.

Tiwaz

Your guiding light is that of action, decisive action, with a heavy slab of honour on top. This may not win you friends, but people will speak of you with respect and, when you are expressing your true self, awe.

This energy is, however, one of self-sacrifice, and if you aren't a paragon to those around you, it will manifest in ways that are detrimental to your evolution. It may even lead to you acting out of someone else's view of what you 'should' be rather than your own vision of yourself. This will hurt, in many and varied ways. Tyr is the god who sacrificed his hand to keep the world safe from Fenrir the wolf. Don't put your hand near wolves. Just saying.

Instead, be active and proud of who you are. Then you'll have lesser folks falling at your feet. People who lead from the front and aren't afraid of hard decisions are few and far between. Stick to your values and you'll be inspirational.

Berkanan

Berkanan is the glow that brings life to the ravaged, and your soul purpose is tied to this frequency of recovery and restoration.

In the frozen mountains of Scandinavia, the first tree to regrow after a fire is the birch. And the bear lives in a cave beneath the snow during the winter. The birch and the bear are representations of the energy that you bring to yourself and those around you.

The ability to help remove toxicity and promote life is your path of heroism. So, removing confusion, helping investments grow and bringing life to abandoned projects is where your energy will flow well.

When you trust your ability to weather the storm by either getting yourself some bear time and keeping yourself warm and cosy or simply recovering faster than anyone else, you harness the recovery frequency of your Sunna rune and can use this to bring restoration to yourself and those around you and enjoy power and success.

Ehwaz

M Ehwaz holds both the energy of companionship and of the horse, and with it as a Sunna rune, your soul mission or heroic self is tied into the energy of companionship and swiftness.

You have the power to be swift – in thought, feeling, body, or some other way – so use it. Leap the chasm. Trust yourself and your tribe. Make a decision and act.

You may be conditioned by life and society, but your ability to think and act in one breath is magic. You are moving while others are dithering, debating and procrastinating. They're still sitting on the sofa when you've done the thing and are enjoying the rewards. Or are off to the next thing. You can happily move from situation to situation, building relationships and having adventures.

You're also able to inspire others and to benefit from their support. Lean into your companions. Not just friends, but companions, for this is the path that leads to victory for you.

Mannaz

Mannaz is the rune of spirit and humanity. This is the energy that will drive a momma to push, or a soldier to risk death to save their buddy. It flows like fire through your veins. Your human spirit, your magic, can influence the world around you. Think Harry Potter. You can be magic like a wizard, or magic like Louise Hay.

Mannaz manifests through your every action. If you choose, you can be a manifesting genius, or an inventive creator, or a compassionate healer. You can channel your spirit through anything you focus on. Even bingeing a boxset. You choose where your spirit flows. It's never wasted, but is it more fun for you to use it in a specific way? Again, you choose. When the chips are down, you have the power.

Mannaz is the human rune, and you, awesome one, bring the power of humanity for all to see, hear and feel.

Laguz

Laguz is the water rune, and water is life, and this energy is what drives your heroic Runic Star Path. One of the magical powers of water is that it is the universal solvent, and everything will eventually dissolve as a result of its movement and power. Laguz brings that energy to you – the gentle power to process away, almost imperceptibly, the injury, the hurt, the toxic, from yourself and/or those you choose to grace with your power. It brings the ability to heal, to wash away sickness.

It also brings life in the form of water itself, and fishing. So, your soul purpose is tied to being able to remove the unwanted, unneeded or blocking, and to the ocean, the massive energy sink that can both hold energy and transmute it into something good.

When life gets difficult, remember that water wears through the most resilient of materials. Use your flowing nature to push through and open the cracks in any situation.

Ingwaz

Ingwaz is the rune of the archetypical hero, the hero's journey and the inner potential we all hold. All we can be, could be, would want to be is held here.

Activating both your own potential and the potential of those around you is what resonates most powerfully with your life path. You can either choose the 'Light the blue touchpaper and walk away' model of activation or the Hagrid/Obi Wan/Aragorn model of guidance.

In life, love and work, look to where you can either activate yourself or, if you choose, those around you. That is, activate into epic awesomeness. No story ever started with 'I was drinking tea quietly at home.' Well, maybe *The Hobbit* came close.

But forget the tea, activate the potential. That is where your power lies. *Potential* is your watchword. Every action you take can expand your experience of the world, so choose to actively participate in life. Choose the adventure.

Othala

With your Sunna energy glowing with Othala vibrations, your life path and focus are linked to family, home and security. Now, it's important to remember that there are many ways that family can manifest. You choose yours. But whatever you choose, look to where you can create the security and harmony that you require in life. This kind of thing may well come easy to you. In fact, building harmony and community may be super easy for you in other situations and settings too, such as work, or teams, or hobbies. It's your solar superpower.

The Othala frequency is also linked to genetics. The rune itself looks a little bit like a primitive DNA helix. So, look to where you can interact with genetics, personal legacies and building heritage and traditions both for yourself and those you love, perhaps by involving yourself in scientific research, families or other groups of people. This is definitely another superpower of yours.

Dagaz

Dagaz energy is one that could be seen as 'hard' or painful, but it's simply part of life. All things change. Time and entropy affect us all. What Dagaz brings through its vibrational magnetism is the cyclic nature of life, the energy of transition, of changing states.

Dagaz itself sits at the end of the runic Furtharc, but it is also at the beginning, as the flow of energy moves forward to Fehu again. With Dagaz as your Sunna rune, use its energies to ease the transition between ending the old and beginning the new. Perhaps you're a great entrepreneur, starting up new businesses, or you have the ability to help people move from addiction to sobriety. Manifesting and actioning change is where your power lies.

Change isn't always pleasant, of course, but remember it is inevitable. You may even find that you ride the cycle of change as a unicycle. While others run in fear.

MANNI RUNE – YOUR EMOTIONAL PURPOSE

The energy of your Manni rune illuminates the emotional path that will help you find peace and contentment in your life. I call this your emotional purpose.

Let's look at how your Manni rune energy shows your emotional purpose.

Fehu

Fehu is the rune of abundance and reputation, and Manni's influence here brings that vibration to your emotional field. Trust your reputation to stand you in good stead when you interact with people. You have the energetic vibration to bring out the best in them and bring an abundance of good fortune and wealth to both your and their emotional experience.

This is definitely an energy of 'Feel it to make it.' Feel the sensations you wish to create and your energy field will bring that energy to you, possibly in the form of money or resources. Or cows. But there are only so many cows most people can cope with. So make sure you are clear on your goals. And your time-scales. As grain takes months to grow, so do dollar bills.

Your energy is one of slow and steady increments. Lots of awesome little interactions will bring you the best results.

Uruz

With the rune of the giant aurochs as your emotional guide, your passions have huge power. Own it. It took a whole tribe to hunt the aurochs, and some of them would not go home. This is how powerful your emotions are. Enjoy your tantrums – I'm guessing no one else does!

Use this unassailable emotional power to fuel your endeavours in life, whatever they may be. Once your passion is engaged, the Uruz energy will trample everything in its way to satiate it.

Uruz energy can be solitary and moody, enjoying its own company. So, take time alone, or you may trample those around you. By accident, of course. It's entirely their own fault.

Above all, remember your emotions and passions are powerful and strong. You're probably the only one who can tame them. So, perhaps, be careful where you point them. Rule them, or let them rule you. Either way, it's going to be an adventure!

Thurizaz

 Thurizaz is an energy of penetration and focus, and neither are Manni's strong suit. Manni loves to stop and stare, but with your laser focus, you can bore past all the distractions straight to the heart of the matter. Your emotional superpower is tied in with being able to feel right into the heart of a situation.

Use this how you will, but you may well find it useful working with people who are hiding things or selling things. Hidden agendas may be an open book to you. Got oracle cards or a rune set? I'd suggest that you modify the messages that come through to you, or they will be a little too cutting to the receiver.

Your cutting words or tongue may well be a tool for righteous rage. Or, after a tequila or two, something you have to apologize for. Find a balance that works for you. And remember, whatever you're told or shown, you know what is hidden beneath. As you can get there straight away.

Ansuz

The energy of Ansuz flowing through Manni the moon is that of the voice, communication and magic. Your voice is your power. Use it however you choose – singing, speaking, whispering or chanting, to name but a few of the ways. Harness the passion within you to amplify your song, your sound, your tone, your frequency. This will build your magical resonance and power.

Your emotions drive this connection to magic and mystery, so ensure that they are fuelling your experience of the world. Passion is a good one to use to direct your power, but so are anger and love, though they are not nearly as consistent. But any emotion married to your voice will lead you to victory and contentment.

Let your voice, your song, your ability to communicate, sing to you, in whatever form you choose to express it. There's power and magic there for you.

Raido

With Raido as your Manni rune, your emotions have the power and the energy to 'go there'. Your inquisitive and adventurous nature is what drives your passion, and there is nothing your emotional power cannot shed light on, no feeling you are unprepared for. Wherever you go and however you get there, you will be able to bring the light of passion, joy and courage with you. And if by chance those feelings aren't there? Well, move on, there's bound to be something fun over there, right?

To do so, you must be resourced, nourished and supported. So, make sure you fill your life with adventure, but remember to nap and explore in dream time too. Manni loves dream time, and this energy is yours too. Filling your life with passion via adventures will allow you to bring a flame of guidance, positivity and growth to even the darkest of situations.

You have this innate power – use it.

Kenaz

Emotional insight and pulse are your guides with Kenaz in your Manni energy. Using your insight and power to 'go there' is a resource that others won't value until they are in need of it. This sucks. But what it does mean is that you have this 'see in the dark' vibe with emotions. Perhaps you resonate with the word 'empath' – or 'badass'. Whatever label you choose to take, or none at all, you're highly sensitive. Be ready with your emotional vibe to provide insights into situations where there is darkness or hidden intent.

Others may get frustrated by your ability to see through their dark night of the soul. But you are a beacon of guidance and emotional light when others are in darkness. Trust your ability to dispel shadows, as this is the way for you to squash fear and shine a light on the path that leads to victory.

Gebo

Emotional connection is your gift to those around you. You're the shoulder to cry on, the friend to rage with, the ally in a fight. If emotions are going there, your energy can add to them. If you choose. Just remember that when you're emotionally invested in something, it's everything to you.

If you're able to be aware of your emotions, you'll be able to gift that understanding to others, be it compassionately, emphatically or intellectually. This will build an emotional relationship that allows you to help those without the emotional gifts you have to share. Your ability to bring the gift of your emotions to any situation is profound. If the party is thumping and *you* are thumping, then *everyone* is having a good time. The reverse is also true.

Use your power wisely, as the gift of your emotional balance, passion and energy can knock those who are less connected off their feet!

Wunjo

Manni is the most easily distracted of gods, pulling the moon around the heavens. Wunjo is the energy of contentment and feeling good. Together, they bring comfort and safety to your emotions. Trust your 'Spidey sense', as this is Wunjo guiding you down paths that lead to being chilled out and calm.

Trust is part of that path. When you trust someone, you get to connect with them on a deep level. In any event, you can tap into others' energies and desires and read what they are feeling. This may not be conscious on your part. And when that energy disrupts your state of calm, there may be explosions.

Wherever you are, make sure that you aim for calmness and contentment. When you do so, you'll be magnetic and potent. When you're out of that alignment, those who knocked you out of it had better run for cover.

Hagalaz

Emotional fall-out is an energy that fills your world when Manni energy attracts Hagalaz vibes. With Hagalaz as your Manni rune, look to the relationships, emotional stimulation and experiences you have in your life, and then you'll be able to take yourself back to the emotional footprint in your soul and fill yourself with power, even though at times you may feel a long way from that.

How do you do it? Whatever situations arise, you're able to use your Hagalaz energy to find the frequency, the learning, that is needed. Especially if the situation is highly emotionally charged. This usually won't apply in the middle of the situation, though, as you'll probably want to bring down hellfire on the entire area instead. Afterwards is when you can apply your power and gain results. Your Hagalaz energy will help you survey what has gone on and make something good from it.

Nauthiz

The energy of Nauthiz and Manni brings several needs to your world. Emotions and actions may need to be simultaneous. Feeling may flow naturally into action, like a hunter of old sighting their prey and raising their bow, or you pressing that app automatically when you open your phone. You have the ability to read situations and respond to them in ways that others may find abrupt or hasty, but you're able to make the intuitive leaps that are needed.

Using your ability to disregard all but the most necessary tasks will bring you success, but also annoy people. You know what is needed, and their thoughts on the matter aren't that relevant. This energy will serve you well in fast-moving environments or situations that require lots of fast adaption. You know where energy needs to flow to get the job done.

Trust your ability to get things done in specific or unconventional ways, as your energy will have spotted something your brain has not.

Isaz

Isaz and Manni bring the ability for you to be super single-minded and focused, with your emotions flowing along one set path, much like a glacier pushing all before it. How you use this focus and directness is up to you, but when you choose to release your emotions, you can move mountains.

Of course, this is super useful when it comes to doing one job or task and not so useful when jumping from task to task.

Also, be aware that Isaz is the rune of ice, and with it as your Manni rune, you may find it all too easy to freeze people out, or indeed freeze them in, especially if you feel they are treating you badly or not behaving the way you expect them to. When you are angry, you can crush people with your stare.

Your cutting wit and temper may also be too sharp sometimes. Remember revenge is deffo not a dish served warm, right?

Jera

Jera is a rune of cycles and harvests, and when it is your Manni rune, your emotional power is fuelled by the seasons around you, the growth, the warm soil and wet earth, the sun, sky and river.

Peaking and dipping as nature's power ebbs and flows is how you express yourself in the world, maybe even feeling the pull of Manni too. Your emotions will flow in cycles – maybe lunar, maybe solar, maybe seasonal.

Becoming aware of your cyclic emotional flow and patterns will bring you increased power and mastery over yourself. Check in with your mind and body as to how you are feeling. Magic flows where your emotions pulse. The cycles of sowing, growing, harvest and rest will dictate where your emotional powers manifest. Pay attention, as this is where your superpowers sit.

Check your personal cycles, daily cycles and monthly cycles. Discover when your emotional power is at its greatest to get the harvest you want.

Eihwaz

With Eihwaz as your Manni rune, emotional power is part of your Runic Star Path. The ability to store and hold the emotive energy of any situation and take it to another time and place is not to be sniffed at.

Emotional stability is something you can choose to cultivate in yourself. And you can bring that energy to those around you just by your presence.

There is another aspect of Eihwaz that can be useful too, that of astral travelling or otherwise connecting with the ethereal realms of the universe. The combination of Manni and Eihwaz will help you, should you choose to build a connection to those around you just by your presence. This is especially useful when tensions or other emotions are high. Moving energy and breaking states and patterns may well be a superpower that you can harness in your life. Or even bringing emotive energy into art and creativity. Look to the emotional energy you can move around.

Peroth

Luck and passion are energies that Peroth brings to your Runic Star Path. With Manni guiding your emotional energy through the lens of Peroth, you have great potential to excel.

You will benefit from trusting your intuition, your emotions and that little twinge in your gut. Spend some time learning how your intuition manifests, as when you are connected to this aspect of yourself, your energy can begin to flow towards the goals you have in life with renewed vigour.

Trust your emotions in all situations, as creativity, luck and fortune will come to you through them. They may not be feelings that others can relate to, but that's not important. With Peroth as your Manni rune, they are definitely powerful for you, so take note of them, trust them and above all act on them. When you act on them, they will bring you opportunity, creativity and luck.

Algiz

Algiz is the rune of edges, barriers and crossing those barriers. What does this mean when it's your Manni rune? You've heard the saying 'How you let people treat you trains them how to treat you'? Well, now you have. Algiz as your Manni rune wants you to have standards for your emotional connections and relationships. It wants you to set boundaries.

Have those standards, set those boundaries. If a person isn't respectful, then they don't deserve your energy or attention. It's as simple as that.

Another expression of your emotional energetic power is to explore the feelings and emotions that are fringe, on the edge, and to challenge accepted wisdom. Go beyond it. Where are the edges that you require for your emotional power to flourish?

With your connection to the other side of the line being so potent, you may also find that stepping over the edge of 'normal' human experience is super easy for you. And why not?

Sowolio

When Sowolio is your Manni rune, your emotions are your guide on your Runic Star Path. When a question comes up in life, don't ask your brain, as your brain will give you some well-reasoned answer, ask your heart, as your heart will guide you better than anything else. This is the magic of Sowolio and Manni.

So, trust your emotions, your feelings and sensations, as you will tend to make the right choices if you go with them. If you go with cold, hard logic, well, yes, it may be 'right', but where's the fun? If you follow your emotions, Sowolio will take you into the adventures that your heart and soul crave.

Bear in mind that with this as your Manni rune, others may find that your ability to read and understand their emotions borders on the supernatural. That is because you are! Use your supernatural emotional knowledge with skill and discernment to grasp victory in life.

Tiwaz

Tiwaz is the rune of action, beliefs and values. Not what you associate with the Moon? Think again. Tiwaz as a Manni rune is passionate and direct, the essence of the warrior poet. Who better to sing epic verse in the mead hall and inspire feats of bravery and honour?

Your focused and honourable approach may not win you friends, but people will speak of you with respect, even awe.

Being a paragon to those around you won't be a conscious choice, but if not realized, this energy will manifest in ways that are detrimental to your evolution, possibly including following someone else's ideals rather than your own. This will hurt, in many and varied ways.

Instead, double down on your passions and your artistic self. Take action in ways that make you feel good. Be proud of yourself. People who lead from the front and are not afraid of hard decisions are few and far between. And you can do this with a song on your lips.

Berkanan

With Berkanan as your Manni rune, you are gifted with the emotional energy of renewal and regeneration. This will offer you solace when things get hard and an extra boost when things are good.

Use this energy to ensure that the storms of life pass you by, as far as possible. Like the bear in winter, you know when to back off and rest if your energy is low. You know how to recover. The birch is the first tree to reappear when the forest has burned down, the first to grow in damaged soil, the first pulse of life in a scorched land. Could finding the wins in situations that seem bleak be one of your skills?

Your energy of birch and bear will serve you when life gets hard, or hectic, or overwhelming. You will instinctively know when to retreat to a 'cave', and when you emerge, your energy will pulse into the world with unparalleled vigour. You have the power to regrow and regenerate after every setback or storm.

Ehwaz

Manni's energy at the time of your birth brings the vibration of Ehwaz, the horse. A horse runs in a herd, and as a human, being part of a team will help you go faster for longer. When you're working and collaborating and moving with others, you're doing what the cosmos breathed into you when you took your first breath.

So, for the best results, utilize the Ehwaz energy of working with a herd of like-minded people. A tribe or team will allow you to more easily access the cosmic frequency that is your

Manni rune. Use the support of others to bolster your mind and body, and support them in turn. It's a two-way street.

Together, a herd survives, and when surrounded by like-minded people, you triumph over everything. Destiny will slide right into your world when you are with your tribe. To achieve fulfilment, don't be an island.

Mannaz

When the soft light of Manni is combined with the rune Mannaz, it brings you energy and power. Emotional energy is Manni's jam. And Mannaz, the human spirit rune, brings that energy in spades.

Manni's influence on your Mannaz vibration brings a powerful connection to the human magic of existence, along with the ability to feel, to have empathy and to take action. A good phrase for this energy is: 'Feel it, do it.'

For you, action is an extension of your felt experience. Perhaps others have called you impulsive? Well, so was Joan of Arc. Mannaz energy is that of the human spirit and the human ability to adapt, overcome and push forward. This vibration fuels your emotional purpose, so you can adapt your emotional energy to fit the situation or environment you find yourself in. It may take some practice, but once you allow that energy to flow, you'll find it's your superpower.

Laguz

Manni's energy at the time of your birth brings the vibration of the rune Laguz, the lake or water. I'm not going to lie, Manni and Laguz bring all the emotions, but also all the healing. You may find your world has a strong emotional undercurrent, with energies flowing to and from your heart.

Because of the watery energy flowing around you, radiance is your key. You will glimmer like light in water, physically and/or energetically. This makes you very attractive to people who need your brand of awesome.

So, Manni and Laguz energy attracts love and devotion, but it's healing and soothing too. The healing can manifest in all kinds of ways. You may be a gifted healer, and if you want to dive into this, look first to water-based or flowing modalities.

In general, think dance, flow and creative processes. All life comes from the ocean and nothing exists without water. Allow life to flow around you and in turn flow around life to find your emotional path.

Ingwaz

Ingwaz is the stereotypical hero, in your case tempered with the softness and liquid-like nature of Manni. Use this heroic energy to flow with the influences around you and adapt to them. Redirect, don't confront. Respond, don't react. The combination of Ingwaz and Manni make for a Muhammad Ali-type energy. 'Float like a butterfly, sting like a bee.' Twenty-one punches dodged has nothing on you.

If someone does sling muck at you or tries to get into an argument with you, when you're channelling this combination of Manni and Ingwaz power, you have already risen above it and left them in your dust. Their wasted energy will only serve to highlight your power.

When you lead, others will follow – not through 'death and glory' energy, but 'Let's get this job done and then the first beer is on me.' Whatever you wish to achieve in life, let your inspirational superpowers flow, as they will lead you to victory.

Othala

When emotional power is vibrating through the rune of Othala in your birth chart, your emotional energy is strengthened and empowered by experiencing life in a place where you feel secure. Othala brings the vibration of security and community, and this energy resonates most strongly when you work with people you value and are in turn valued by.

Enhance your emotional stability and strength by leaning back into the energies of your family and friends. You can even make yourself a nexus of those energies, the point through which all interaction and stimulation flow in a group of people. This will reward you by making your energy a safe space for you to interact with others in.

With this safe energy, others will unconsciously be drawn to you, as you provide the stability and security they crave. And so you in turn can build a supportive community around yourself and enjoy the feeling of security.

Dagaz

Dagaz is the initiator, and when this is your Manni rune, you can use your connection with your emotions and those around you to aid in the initiation of change. Yours. Theirs. Anyone's. You can use your words and/or magic to powerful effect by helping others change their opinions, feelings and entrenched ideas.

This magic is best used softly, just as the day dawns and sets with gentle poise and power. Hard edges of change can disrupt others' energy pathways.

Don't be too hard on yourself, either. I know it's your default. Dagaz sees all the options, but you only need to take one, not and *never* all of them. When you make a decision, stick to it and let your energy flow that way. Ride the wave, no matter how many shiny things present themselves to distract you. Don't get thrown by ideas of what could be. Stay the course and you will find fulfilment.

JORD RUNE – YOUR PRACTICAL PURPOSE

Your Jord rune is a practical Runic Star Path for you to follow. I call this energy your practical purpose. It leans into the practical aspects of your life, those areas where you can make sure things work how you want them to work.

Let's look at how your Jord rune reveals ways to go about it.

Fehu

Fehu, the energy of abundance. When this is your Jord rune, this is an abundance of whatever you choose – smiles, euros, gold, food, babies.... You're supremely placed to use both the Momma Goddess energy of the Earth and the warm glow of Sunna to ensure there is plenty for all your kin. Creating abundance in all its forms will be a practical and focused life path for you to follow.

What do you get when the sun shines on the fertile Earth? Harvest. You bring that energy to projects and endeavours. Your ability to make even the most barren space produce the resources needed is your superpower. Just let it happen. If you try too hard... well, you know what they say about perfect ponytails. Simply trust your superpower to bring projects, courses or whatever it is you are working on to fruition.

Uruz

With Uruz as your Jord rune, the momma energy of Jord is giving you the power of Uruz – the power, the strength, the ability to withstand all that is thrown at you.

Uruz is strength – gym strength as well as strength of will. Being able to bring your strength, however it manifests, to a situation is how you achieve victory. When you let your powers flow, nothing and no one can stand in your way. Don't play polite with this energy, or it will wander off into the mists, leaving you with a tame milk cow, rather than a primal ox with horns that can destroy a village. Own your ability to be strong and resilient. People might as well get used to the fact that you can crush them energetically with your will.

Being super strong can exhaust you, of course. So make sure you take time to be alone to recharge your batteries.

Thurizaz

With Thurizaz as your Jord rune, your practical purpose is, simply put, to get straight to the point. You want more?

The point of the thorn is your watchword here. Make things as simple as possible, as uncomplicated as possible and as direct as possible. If you remove complexity and confusion from your world, your life will be better for it. As will the lives of those around you. Looking for the direct path or direction is going to make you feel and act with more power and verve. Keeping it simple and straightforward will make your life and plans much more enjoyable and efficient. Efficient is good, right?

While working on a project, make sure that there is a clear focus and intent. Without that, you are likely to feel lost and undervalued. The same goes for doing magical things – make sure that you are focused. If not, your powerful gaze will lose its energy trying to do everything.

Ansuz

Ansuz is the energy of speech and inspiration – god voice energy. In Old English the Ansuz rune was Os, meaning 'god'. With this as your Jord rune, your practical purpose will be tied up neatly with your ability to communicate clearly and get your point across.

Ansuz energy will also allow you to find inspiration in the most mundane things. And to inspire even the gloomiest energies – and people.

Your own inspiration will come from things that are tied with your passions and focus and, as this is your Earth rune, perhaps from the rise and fall of the oceans, from the mountains and the woodlands. So you can bring your innate ability to be inspired and communicate to your everyday experience of life, wherever you happen to be.

In fact, your greatest ally is your ability to talk yourself into and out of any situation, inspiring emotions in others as you go.

Raido

With Raido, the rune of adventure and exploration, as your Jord rune, your practical purpose is tied with adventure. Do you find it hard to stay in one place for long? Why are you even there anyway, when there's something on the other side of the hill – and wait, is that another hill?

Given the chance, your basic energy will happily flow into an adventure, any adventure, be it exploring the unknown or making mundane tasks for your team exciting. The military life may call you. So will any challenge. For you, seeing new places may make any challenge worthwhile.

Picture the van-life experience, or overlanding, or even the long highway to somewhere, anywhere. Doesn't that make you feel good? When you experience life as an adventure, you release all the power within you.

So, always choose adventure. That way you'll never be bored and your passions will flow with purpose and power.

Kenaz

Kenaz is the rune of light, the torch in the darkness, the flame chasing away the fear. As Jord, the mother goddess, is rooting this power into you, whatever you do, do it with the intent of bringing light and knowledge to the world.

In Old English, the *cunninga* was the cunning woman, the witch. The cunning helm became the crown of the cunning man, the king. Kenaz is the root energy of both these archetypes. So, use your connection to yourself and your connection to the world to bring knowledge and light to all those you want to illuminate. Remember, part of the wisdom of shining the light is choosing where you point it. It can be laser focused or shining over everyone like the sun. You choose.

Whatever you choose, you have the power to chase darkness away, or let it in and direct it as you wish. That's your choice too.

Gebo

Practically, with Gebo as your guide, you have the gift of the gift, the ability to make sure that your needs are met by making sure that others' needs are met. The Runic Star Path that Gebo leads you down is one of feeling into where you can meet others' needs and where they can meet yours. Not a tit-for-tat kind of energy, more that how you choose to gift your energy, whether that be in the form of money, work, listening or something else, will determine the energetic response.

Keep in mind that gifting makes a twist in the *Wyrd*, the web of fate, and by giving your energy, you link yourself with that of the receiver. Your personal vibration will bring the receiver slightly more into alignment with your energy. So, part of your practical purpose is levelling up people with your innate power.

Wunjo

 Wunjo is the essence of contentment, of bliss. You know that feeling of yumminess when everything is as it should be, you are warm and cosy and the drink is just right, and no one will bother you? That is Wunjo.

With Wunjo as your Jord rune, you're working towards that energy, working to make yourself content. Bringing that energy to those around you is your superpower. You can put people at ease in any situation and utilize this skill any way you want, be it talking someone round or calming someone down. Whatever you choose to do, your ability to make people feel loved and content will flow easily from you.

Wunjo energy also recharges you when you are depleted. You draw your power from being warm and fuzzy and from making sure the resources are in place to be warm and fuzzy in the future. This practical element of Wunjo is great when it comes to making your way in the world.

Hagalaz

When Jord brings the Runic Star Path of Hagalaz to you, look to what your passion pulls you to do, as your practical purpose is really tied with your passion. With Hagalaz energy, you may well find yourself in a role that sorts out problems. Just remember that a scorched earth approach is not the way forward for all the problems in the world!

Remember that hail hurts when it falls, and when your power to change things really starts flowing, then those in the way may get crushed. It may well be their own fault, but....

The ability to thrive and excel when everything around you is changing and growing is part of your path. Perhaps high-stress environments are your jam? Emergency workers or recovery teams? Or planning for rebuilding after everything has changed.

This innate urge to let things go and restart after learning the lessons will serve you well in life. Just don't set fire to everything, okay?

Nauthiz

Nauthiz is the rune of need, of the pulse to survive. When it is your Jord rune, this energy flows through you and helps you connect to those around you. This is where your practical purpose and skills will reside.

Jord, the Earth, wants you to be aware of what needs to be done, felt and spoken. Meeting this need will give you purpose and drive.

This isn't to say that you are a saviour to others, or a slave to their needs, though at times the needs of others may supersede your own, or indeed yours may supersede theirs. This is an important distinction to make, because if you're tapped out, you'll burn out. Make sure the needs you attempt to meet are ones that fill you up, not tear you down. This is a vital lesson for you, and the earlier you learn it, the better. But by giving your energy to the needs you wish to meet, you will find infinite power and fulfilment.

Isaz

Isaz as your Jord rune gives you the potential for endless patience and huge power – the power to grind down even the most stubborn of wills. Ever been called stubborn yourself? Well, this is where that comes from. You're as stubborn as an ice floe.

Looking to where you're doing you is the way forward. Take note of this, as it will be somewhere you could excel in the world. And remember that distracting others with your wit, glamour and beauty while getting the job done is deffo a superpower. Yours.

Practically, look to where you can maximize this ability to skate over obstacles or distract naysayers while getting your needs met in the most potent way possible – the way that works best for you. While you're doing this, don't worry about being abrasive. The results will speak for themselves. Glacial valleys are the most fertile in the world.

Jera

 Your practical purpose is wrapped around the rune of Jera, the rune of harvest and rewards. Everyone likes getting rewards. Why is this special for you?

Well, the energy of Jera hinges on doing the work to get the best harvest. You give nothing, you get nothing, right? Making sure that the right things are done at the right time to get the required result is a manifestation of Jera energy. And speaking of manifesting, you are an expert manifester.

How do you do it? You manifest though the energetic lens of making sure everything is in place to bring about the manifestation. Others may miss steps, but you'll make sure they're all completed, even though you may not consciously think about it.

Natural cycles are your friend here. Doing winter work at the height of summer won't produce the best results. Trust your nature to guide you as to when to plant and when to enjoy the harvest.

Eihwaz

Eihwaz as a Jord rune brings the power to store and control energy, and this is part of your practical purpose and power in life. Be it practically with electrics or fire, or in more esoteric ways like energy healing or things of an oracular nature, this is an area in which you will excel.

The path of practical energy storage is one of choosing to be where the energy you want exists, be it in the form of people, animals or work. Choose the environments where you can fill up on the energy you need. Then you can take that energy to other places, people and environments.

Environments are important to you. Focus on the feeling of any environment that you find yourself in. That way you can choose whether to pick up the energies or not.

Talismans or crystals may aid you in this. But you're the one with the power.

Peroth

Jord loves things to be practical and applicable and grounded in the Earth. The creativity energy that Peroth brings is very Jord, a very practical pathway. Working in a creative environment would be inspiring for you and a powerful way of expressing yourself and fulfilling your practical purpose.

The luck of Peroth is a different feeling. It flows. But trust your instincts and that little feeling. Because it's the energy of the universe giving you a little hint.

The luck you act on may not be 'good' luck. It may not feel good at the time, or indeed for 20 years. In itself, luck isn't good or bad, it's just the energy of the fates. The magic for you is working where you can improve the situations you find yourself in by acting on your luck. Your Runic Star Path is one where you can create opportunities for yourself. So, trust yourself. Trust your luck. For opportunities can lead to victory.

Algiz

Algiz brings a complex energy to your Runic Star Path. (I'm sure you enjoyed reading that.) It adds edges to your experience and the ability to adapt and overcome, Bear Grylls style, but hopefully without drinking urine.

Your ability to walk the edges of life, to see where one thing starts and another ends, is a power that is both useful and a pain. Unless you're careful, you can fall into the unknown. This is okay, though, as you can adapt to new situations and extend your edges to cope with new experiences.

You can use your ability to find edges and build barriers when working with others too. Especially those who need, or try to leach, your capable energy.

Don't be afraid to adapt your thinking to new situations, as your Jord energy really wants you to flow into victory through expanding experiences. This may be by working in fields where the ability to adapt while maintaining strong boundaries is required. Like the emergency services or crisis management.

Sowolio

When your practical purpose is linked with Sowolio, the rune of the sun, navigation and guidance are the energies you have to work with. Even if you don't wish it, people will be energetically drawn to follow your guidance, your example, your path.

Feel into the ways you can use this to achieve your goals in life. Practically, you'll probably find that situations where people are being foolish, or inefficient with energy, especially yours, will cause you to lose your cool. A cool that is probably a little too close to being lost in any event.

More positively, you are a leader, an inspirer, a thought leader. Let your art, creativity and passion lead you into a happy and creative life. One that sees your light showing the way. This urge to lead, to inspire, will serve you. Just be aware that leading from the front, while being your jam, may open you up to attack, perhaps from behind. Keep your cool, okay?

Tiwaz

Tiwaz as your Jord rune brings a powerful energy of action based on values and beliefs. It brings that 'Less talking, more doing' feeling to life. Your energy wants to be doing things, either with your mind or with your body. Choosing to act will always have a favourable feeling for you. And constant meetings? They'll probably have you climbing the walls!

Look to ways you can choose action over inaction. Perhaps you're a great innovator, or inventor, or entrepreneur. Or your world is improved in some way through the energy of being first. However you choose to express this aspect of yourself, know that your creativity and passion will become clearer and more focused as you take action.

Even if you're plagued by anxiety or doubt, know that moving towards a goal that is in alignment with your values and beliefs will always make life better for you.

Berkanan

When your Jord rune is Berkanan, the energies of the birch and the bear are coming to you through the Earth Mother. Jord is grounded, relaxed, and can take all that we throw at her and still love us. Berkanan has the power to withstand the storm, the fire and the winter, not through toughing it out, but through getting underground and staying there. What does this mean in practical terms?

Your practical purpose is to make sure you and those you care about aren't at risk when disaster strikes. Not through hiding, but by being resourced – energetically, emotionally, physically and practically. The bear has energy stores in its fat. The birch has sweet sap and fertile seeds, as well as the ability to turn toxicity into nourishment thanks to the mycelium that live on its roots.

Trust your ability to weather the firestorm by getting out of the way, and then, when it's over, to heal and transform the energy around you.

Ehwaz

Jord, the Earth, is grounded and relaxed, and Ehwaz, horse energy, excels at working with others. So, when Ehwaz is your Jord rune and the proverbial hits the fan, which it inevitably will, you know you've got this.

What you bring to the table is the reassurance of being firmly grounded in the real. Your companionship and kindness are super comforting to those around you and, like a horse, you will run long and hard, and always with purpose. For example, a drive for driving's sake is not for you, but hitting that store in the next city or perhaps going to see some awesome trees will make it worthwhile.

In fact, you have the ability to make even the most mystical feel practical. This may aggravate more esoteric people. But don't worry. The woollier-thinking people you love will get where they are going. And because of you they'll have fuel in the car, a bug-out bag in the boot and probably snacks in the glove box too.

Mannaz

Your practical purpose is what grounds you in the world, and in your case it is linked with Mannaz, the rune of the human spirit. So, should you wish, you can move your spirit in practical ways – ways that open up energetic pathways to help yourself and others through the power that you bring.

This is likely to be structured power. Mannaz loves structure. Take care not to get stuck in rigid ways of thinking, though. Structure is great, but flowing around, through and in it is where your real power can be found.

You have the ability to manifest physical rewards for yourself if you choose to make it so, but don't let that be the main focus of your energy.

People will be drawn to you for your ability to be practical and stable. Let them come, as you will grow because of it. And so will they.

Laguz

With Laguz as your Jord rune, the Great Momma is calling you, telling you that you have depths to explore, power to draw on when needed, and energy and mystery to bring to the lives of those around you.

When all around you are depleted, lost or out of their depth, you have the energetic vibration to find connection, grounding and a way forward in even the most unpredictable of circumstances.

Bringing healing, or life itself, is also one of your practical gifts. The healing doesn't have to be in the form of bandages or herbs. The mere vibration of your presence can help others to shift their perspective, change their behaviour and heal their wounds, washing away all the negative and leaving just clarity behind.

Trust your depths, even if you don't actually know how deep you go, and know that anyone making waves for you will reap the tsunami.

Ingwaz

Jord is the Great Momma of Midgard and you are the hero, Ingwaz. When you're seen for the amazingness that you are, when people are awed by your sheer brilliance, you're expressing what the cosmos breathed into you when you took your first breath.

Ingwaz is the stereotypical hero, and your hero archetype is rooted firmly in the rock and earth of the Great Momma, so you can literally crush your naysayers in order to be seen in your radiant glory.

Your ability to stand out from the crowd will fuel your sense of correctness, your passions and your sense of self. Don't be afraid to take the path that makes others question you and to carry on regardless. That's what heroes do.

When you do the things that make you happy, people will look at you in awe and speak of you in hushed tones. Your ability to be seen and to see the hero's path before you is what makes you the powerful human that you are.

Othala

The Great Momma Jord is super practical and likes to get stuff done. She brings you Othala energy to get that stuff done so that those around you are supported and safe. That will bring you support and stability too.

With this vibration comes freedom, which stimulates your creativity. When you're with people you trust and in a place where you feel secure, you'll find it easy to create, work or otherwise be awesome. Working from home may be the best thing that has ever happened to you.

Making sure all around you are feeling free and uninhibited will help you really get your life mission going. Because as their energy rises, yours reaches new heights. However, free and uninhibited people can be really annoying, especially when living and working together. So make sure there are some boundaries in place.

Make your home your super-comfortable fortress and lean into your community too, and you will be both powerful and productive.

Dagaz

 Dagaz is the rune of initiation, and with this as your Jord rune, your practical purpose is to initiate yourself and those who are drawn to you.

Initiation doesn't have to be walking for 40 days across a desert or hanging from a tree. It can be the soft questioning of long-held beliefs, the permission slip to be different. Your heroic purpose is to softly – or harshly, as you decide – initiate yourself and others into new paradigms of life and experience.

Dagaz energy will help you change minds, opinions and beliefs to aid the expansion of your family and the collective. This is a superpower that you can use however you like in your world.

Utilizing this skill will help you in work, life and love, as people will be attracted to you when they need to be initiated. The skill here lies in keeping yourself fulfilled and happy and not being constantly surrounded by people sucking your energy to 'up-level' themselves. Strong boundaries will bring you joy.

The resonance of the runes flows from the world tree at the galactic centre. This is the source of runic frequencies.

Chapter 6

Exploring Runic Resonance

The Norns provide us with energy and direction as we emerge into the world. They put things on our path that we can act on to create the world we desire. Some things are hard to get, but others are as easy as breathing. This is how we know we are on a path that will fulfil us. If we are constantly struggling, then we aren't picking up what the universe is putting down.

Or, and here's the kicker, we've not told the Norns what we want in a language that they can understand.

SPEAKING TO THE NORNS

Our Runic Star Path is the language of the Norns. It's how they speak to us and through us, and how we can speak to them. And the language of the universe is the language of cause and effect. When we do something, something else happens in response.

Knowing this gives us real power. You know when you order a burger from that place down the road, you get a good burger, but the pizza isn't so good and you don't like it. So you don't order it. That way, you get the good burger, right?

It's the same with the universe and the Norns. You speak to them in a way they understand and you don't ask for what you don't want and you do ask for what you do want. Otherwise you'll just get the default energies that are simply lying around. Like the rubbish pizza.

This is where we can delve into your Runic Star Path. The runic energies there are a key, a lexicon, a Rosetta stone to your soul. To what you really want.

So, more lists, but this time lists of associations, with the aim of providing more information on the energies of the runes so you can deepen your connection to them and experiment with expressing your wishes and bringing the energies you want into your life.

These associations are:

✦ Dates: The dates the rune energy appears in the calendar.

✦ Degrees: The degrees of the rune on the birth chart.

✦ Totems: Animism energies that are like the runic energy.

✦ Colours: Colours that resonate with the rune.

✦ Crystals: Crystals that work well with the rune.

✦ Connection frequency: The brainwave frequency of the rune.

✦ Transmission frequency: The musical frequency of the rune.

✦ Element: The element associated with the rune.

✦ Ruler: The god/goddess/planet that has influence over the rune (more on this in Chapter 9).

✦ Keywords: Words to help you connect to the rune.

You can get as creative with these as you wish, perhaps making altarpieces, or jewellery, or soundscapes for each rune. If you want to connect to Fehu, perhaps with a crystal, then iron pyrite is a great way to do so. Or how about charging water to bring Fehu energy into your cup of tea in the morning? You can play it the G# note with the intention of bringing Fehu energy into the water. And then place the teapot on a Fehu rune.

Perhaps colours are your bag? They aren't mine – I'm colour-blind. But I can say that writing Fehu on a gold card will bring that energy in. And you can charge it in your sleep using the brainwave pattern at 10 Hz (Alpha).

To build an altar to a rune you can also use totems of the gods who have influence over that rune. Freya, for instance, again for Fehu.

Really allow yourself to get to know each rune, remembering that these are my interpretations, and as you start to work and weave with them, you may create and sense your own, and that's totally okay too. I want you to work, and play, with the tools that work best for you. I've got a friend who is a world-class cellist, and he connects to the runes through music.

And, as we love to see how we can make connections with others, there is a runic compatibility element here too. This is great for exploring your relationships with others. I've provided Sunna rune interactions here, but this isn't the be-all and end-all of relationship building, so look more deeply into how the energies work together. A Fehu Sunna energy person will probably get on well with a Manni Eihwaz person, as the controlled emotions in Manni help direct the raw power in Fehu. So they won't end up spending all the resources on kittens.

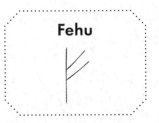

Fehu

+ Dates: 21 June–7 July (from midday to midday)

+ Degrees: 0–15 degrees Cancer

+ Totems: Cow, grain

+ Colours: Gold

+ Crystals: Iron pyrite

+ Connection frequency: 10 Hz (Alpha)

+ Transmission frequency: 210.42 Hz (G#)

+ Element: Fire

+ Ruler: Freya (Venus)

+ Keywords: Wealth, abundance, reputation

Runic compatibility

✓ Fehu works well with Wunjo and Berkanan. Relationships between them will be abundant and creative. Fehu brings abundance to Wunjo's comfort, and warmth to Berkanan's cave.

✕ Fehu does not work well with Eihwaz, as one grows and the other controls.

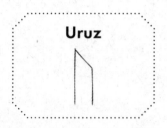

Uruz

✦ Dates: 7–23 July (from midday to midday)

✦ Degrees: 16–30 degrees Cancer

✦ Totems: Ox

✦ Colours: Dirt brown, red ochre

✦ Crystals: Iron

✦ Connection frequency: 10 Hz (Alpha)

✦ Transmission frequency: 126.22 Hz (B)

✦ Element: Earth

✦ Ruler: Sunna (the Sun)

✦ Keywords: Strength, power, stubbornness

Runic compatibility

✓ Uruz gets on best with Hagalaz and Ehwaz. The power and endurance of Uruz bring the stability Hagalaz lacks, and Ehwaz and Uruz rock each other's worlds through the power Uruz brings to the valued companionship.

✗ Uruz isn't a fan of Peroth — this less grounded rune jars Uruz's solidity.

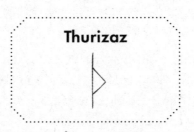

Thurizaz

✦ Dates: 23 July–7 August (from midday to midday)

✦ Degrees: 0–15 degrees Leo

✦ Totems: Thorn, spear

✦ Colours: Mahogany

✦ Crystals: Garnet

✦ Connection frequency: 10 Hz (Alpha)

✦ Transmission frequency: 126.22 Hz (B)

✦ Element: Water

✦ Ruler: Thor (Jupiter)

✦ Keywords: Focus, cutting, sharpness

Runic compatibility

✓ Thurizaz is a supporter rune, providing focus and movement to others. Its direction and focus lift Nauthiz up, and Nauthiz, by its very nature, is magnetic to Thurizaz. Mannaz and Thurizaz also get on, through the energizing nature of Thurizaz and Mannaz's power of sub-state energy. They do awesome things together.

✗ Thurizaz and Algiz don't get on, as Thurizaz is movement and energy, whereas Algiz is static and likes an edge, a boundary. The still and contemplative Algiz gets wound up by Thurizaz's penetrating nature.

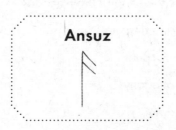

Ansuz

✦ Dates: 7–23 August (from midday to midday)

✦ Degrees: 16–30 degrees Leo

✦ Totems: The mouth, words

✦ Colours: Sky blue

✦ Crystals: Aquamarine

✦ Connection frequency: 10 Hz (Alpha)

✦ Transmission frequency: 141.27 Hz (C#)

✦ Element: Air

✦ Ruler: Odin (Mercury)

✦ Keywords: Communication, words, leadership

Runic compatibility

✓ Ansuz is a powerful rune, as it's Odin's favourite. It gets on well with Isaz and Laguz. Isaz is a good match for Ansuz, as each rune loves to tie the other in playful knots of language, light and confusion. Laguz and Ansuz are also a good match, as the words of magic spoken through Ansuz can be used by Laguz to power its healing.

✗ Ansuz does not get on well with Sowolio, as Ansuz is in charge and knows the way, and Sowolio knows that it is right. Who will lead and who will follow?

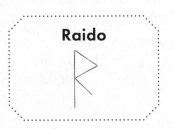

Raido

✦ Dates: 23 August–8 September (from midday to midday)

✦ Degrees: 0–15 degrees Virgo

✦ Totems: Hills, the explorer

✦ Colours: Grass green

✦ Crystals: Moonstone

✦ Connection frequency: 10 Hz (Alpha)

✦ Transmission frequency: 141.27 Hz (C#)

✦ Element: Fire

✦ Ruler: Odin (Mercury)

✦ Keywords: Adventure, curiosity, mobility

Runic compatibility

✓ Raido works well with Jera and Ingwaz. Relationships here will bring adventure and new discoveries. Raido helps Jera not to be rooted in one place and helps Ingwaz to develop in other directions.

✗ Raido does not work well with Tiwaz, as one wants to walk the path of responsibility, while the other wants to play on the other side of the hill.

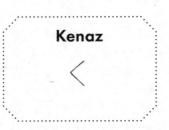

Kenaz

+ Dates: 8–23 September (from midday to midday)

+ Degrees: 16–30 degrees Virgo

+ Totems: Torch, fire

+ Colours: Fire yellow

+ Crystals: Ruby

+ Connection frequency: 9 Hz (Alpha)

+ Transmission frequency: 221.23 Hz (G#)

+ Element: Earth

+ Ruler: Freya (Venus)

+ Keywords: Self-belief, self-discovery, light in the darkness

Runic compatibility

✓ Kenaz brings light and inspiration to Eihwaz, allowing it to grow. Kenaz also brings power and hope to Othala, allowing it to step beyond what is known.

✗ Kenaz does not get on with Berkanan, as Berkanan likes to be hidden, while Kenaz likes to be seen!

Gebo

- ✦ Dates: 23 September–8 October (from midday to midday)
- ✦ Degrees: 0–15 degrees Libra
- ✦ Totems: Gifts, presents, respect
- ✦ Colours: Soft blue, off-white
- ✦ Crystals: Star ruby
- ✦ Connection frequency: 9 Hz (Alpha)
- ✦ Transmission frequency: 221.23 Hz (G#)
- ✦ Element: Water
- ✦ Ruler: Freya (Venus)
- ✦ Keywords: Gifts, respect, mutual support

Runic compatibility

✓ Gebo's energy of exchanging gifts to build respect is drawn to Peroth and Dagaz. Peroth's sexy, lucky nature is a natural companion to Gebo, as respect is important with sex and love, and especially with building *Hamingja*. Dagaz and Gebo also get on well, as the changing energies Dagaz brings suit Gebo's flow into new situations and connections.

✗ Gebo and Ehwaz are troublesome for each other, as the implicit trust Ehwaz brings is more intimate than the demonstrated respect of Gebo. They are not incompatible, but approach the same thing from different directions. And they don't pay attention to each other.

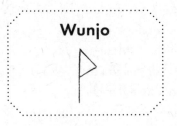

Wunjo

+ Dates: 8–23 October (from midday to midday)

+ Degrees: 16–30 degrees Libra

+ Totems: Fluffy blankets, full wood store

+ Colours: Baby blue

+ Crystals: Golden beryl

+ Connection frequency: 3 Hz (Delta)

+ Transmission frequency: 140.25 Hz (C#)

+ Element: Air

+ Ruler: Myrmir (Pluto)

✦ Keywords: Bliss, contentment, working towards those goals

Runic compatibility

✓ Wunjo is a fairly easy-going energy, once it has sat down on the sofa. Algiz and Fehu are good matches for it – Algiz, as Wunjo likes a blanket fort and Algiz likes making the fort, and Fehu, as it brings abundance for Wunjo to consume, wrapped in a burrito. Fehu likes providing.

✗ Wunjo doesn't get on too well with Mannaz. There are elements of Mannaz in Wunjo, namely getting the snug built, but that's it. Mannaz likes to rush and create and manifest and do human stuff. Wunjo is fine with that, 'Just don't do it near me, I'm chilling out.'

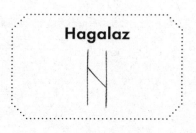

Hagalaz

✦ Dates: 23 October–7 November (from midday to midday)

✦ Degrees: 0–15 degrees Scorpio

✦ Totems: Hail

✦ Colours: Bruise black/blue

+ Crystals: Mookaite

+ Connection frequency: 3 Hz (Delta)

+ Transmission frequency: 140.25 Hz (C#)

+ Element: Fire

+ Ruler: Myrmir (Pluto)

+ Keywords: Change, renewal, surprise

Runic compatibility

✓ While not working well with anyone, Hagalaz tolerates Sowolio and Uruz more than most. Their relationship will be one of change and evolution, whether they like it or not. The combination of Sowolio and Hagalaz brings a potent energy of walking a path to new horizons while the path is collapsing. And Uruz brings strength and endurance, which Hagalaz doesn't have a lot of.

✗ Hagalaz is quite antagonistic in general, but with Laguz the energy is more akin to a pyroclastic burst. Think Eyjafjallajökull (Ey-a-fee-alla-yock-ul) eruption.

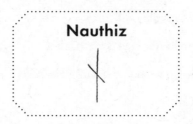

Nauthiz

+ Dates: 7–22 November (from midday to midday)

+ Degrees: 16–30 degrees Scorpio

+ Totems: The heart

+ Colours: Black

+ Crystals: Obsidian

+ Connection frequency: 7 Hz (Alpha)

+ Transmission frequency: 183.53 Hz (F#)

+ Element: Earth

+ Ruler: Thor (Jupiter)

+ Keywords: Need, requirements, basics

Runic compatibility

✓ Nauthiz is a very clingy energy that grasps and holds, but it works well with several runes. The direction and focus of Tiwaz bring it into alignment, and Thurizaz helps Nauthiz focus on what it needs. Both Tiwaz and Thurizaz like to look after others, and Nauthiz needs this.

✗ Nauthiz and Ingwaz don't work well together, though, as Ingwaz wants to grow and expand, while Nauthiz wants to stay put.

+ Dates: 22 November–7 December (from midday to midday)

+ Degrees: 0–15 degrees Sagittarius

+ Totems: Ice

+ Colours: Iceberg blue, crystal clear

+ Crystals: Clear quartz

+ Connection frequency: 7 Hz (Alpha)

+ Transmission frequency: 183.53 Hz (F#)

+ Element: Water

+ Ruler: Thor (Jupiter)

+ Keywords: Glamour, distraction, smoothness

Runic compatibility

✓ Isaz gets on well with Berkanan and Ansuz. With the power of Isaz, Berkanan is able to endure and recover much more quickly, and Ansuz loves the glamour and sparkle Isaz brings, while Isaz loves Ansuz's wordplay.

✗ Isaz and Othala don't get on. Othala wants to build warmth and family connectivity, while Isaz is cold and frozen. Independent even, though more through circumstances than choice. Still, quite the opposite end of the energetic spectrum.

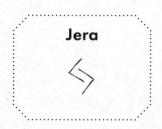

Jera

✦ Dates: 7–22 December (from midday to midday)

✦ Degrees: 16–30 degrees Sagittarius

✦ Totems: The year, harvest

✦ Colours: Deep forest green

✦ Crystals: Citrine

✦ Connection frequency: 6 Hz (Theta)

✦ Transmission frequency: 147.85 Hz (D)

✦ Element: Air

✦ Ruler: Loki (Saturn)

✦ Keywords: Harvest, fruitfulness, hard work

Runic compatibility

✓ Jera's powerful harvest energy gels well with Ehwaz and Raido. Jera loves to make sure things happen at the right time, and Ehwaz will move heaven and Earth to make them happen. Raido and Jera work well, as Jera likes to be able to expand its energies to bring more harvest, and Raido likes to see what is on the other side of the hill.

✗ Jera and Dagaz don't get on. Jera likes things to happen on schedule, whereas Dagaz likes things to happen, full stop. With no regard to Jera's plans or timetable.

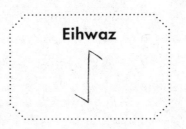

Eihwaz

✦ Dates: 22 December–6 January (from midday to midday)

✦ Degrees: 16–30 degrees Capricorn

✦ Totems: Yew tree

+ Colours: Berry red

+ Crystals: Selenite

+ Connection frequency: 6 Hz (Theta)

+ Transmission frequency: 147.85 Hz (D)

+ Element: Fire

+ Ruler: Loki (Saturn)

+ Keywords: Travelling through dimensions, changing states, holding energy

Runic compatibility

✓ Eihwaz's stabilizing energy works well with Mannaz and Kenaz. Mannaz is a Water rune (for the elements, see Chapter 8), and the combination of Fire and Water is often poor, but Eihwaz is designed to weather the Water, and adds heat to the human spirit, while bringing longevity to the exploration of Kenaz.

✗ Eihwaz doesn't work well with Fehu – while one grows, the other controls.

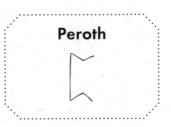

Peroth

+ Dates: 6–20 January (from midday to midday)

+ Degrees: 16–30 degrees Capricorn

+ Totems: Dice cup, womb

+ Colours: Lip pink

+ Crystals: Carnelian

+ Connection frequency: 6 Hz (Theta)

+ Transmission frequency: 147.85 Hz (D)

+ Element: Earth

+ Ruler: Loki (Saturn)

+ Keywords: Luck, sex, chance

Runic compatibility

✓ Laguz and Peroth are a good match, as are Peroth and Gebo. Laguz helps Peroth feel nurtured. Gebo helps Peroth keep its self-respect while being itself.

✗ Peroth and Uruz don't work too well, as Uruz is solid, whereas Peroth is anything but. Rock vs sand.

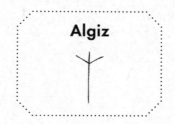

Algiz

+ Dates: 20 January–4 February (from midday to midday)

+ Degrees: 1–15 degrees Aquarius

+ Totems: Elk antlers, shield wall

+ Colours: Antler brown

+ Crystals: Kyanite

+ Connection frequency: 6 Hz (Theta)

+ Transmission frequency: 147.85 Hz (D)

+ Element: Water

+ Ruler: Loki (Saturn)

+ Keywords: Boundaries, defence, standards

Runic compatibility

✓ Algiz gets on well with Ingwaz and Wunjo. Ingwaz wants to grow everywhere and Algiz wants to make sure there are some edges and focus, so both are contained and grow with some semblance of order. Wunjo and Algiz work well together too, as Wunjo likes to be cosy in one place and Algiz likes to be able to keep things safe.

x Algiz does not get on so well with Thurizaz, as they tend to work at cross purposes. Thurizaz moves around a lot, whereas Algiz likes to be still and have boundaries.

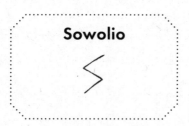

Sowolio

+ Dates: 4–19 February (from midday to midday)

+ Degrees: 16–30 degrees Aquarius

+ Totems: The sun

+ Colours: Bright yellow

+ Crystals: Crystal calcite

+ Connection frequencies: 6 Hz (Theta) and 4 Hz (Theta)

+ Transmission frequencies: 147.85 Hz (D), 211.44 Hz (G#)

+ Element: Air

+ Ruler: Sunna (the Sun)

+ Keywords: Guidance, pathways, direction

Runic compatibility

✓ Sowolio works well with Hagalaz and Othala. Its energy of guidance is actually compatible with Hagalaz, as a path will be clear once Hagalaz has flattened everything. Its clear direction is also useful to Othala, as Othala likes to know what's going on.

✗ Sowolio and Ansuz are not the best suited of energies, as Ansuz likes to develop new ideas by leaving the path and Sowolio *is* the path.

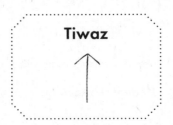

Tiwaz

✦ Dates: 19 February–5 March (from midday to midday)

✦ Degrees: 0–15 degrees Pisces

✦ Totems: Spear, sword, one arm

✦ Colours: Violet

✦ Crystals: Amber

✦ Connection frequency: 4 Hz (Theta)

✦ Transmission frequency: 211.44 Hz (G#)

+ Element: Fire

+ Ruler: Tyr (Mars)

+ Keywords: Honour, leadership, doing the right thing

Runic compatibility

✓ Tiwaz's honour and action energy work well in pacifying Nauthiz and empowering Dagaz. Nauthiz needs direction to satiate its need and hunger, and with the values of Tiwaz, Dagaz flows more confidently into a new state.

✗ Tiwaz does not work well with Raido, as Tiwaz wants to walk the path of responsibility, while Raido wants to play on the other side of the hill.

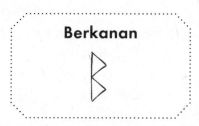

Berkanan

+ Dates: 5–20 March (from midday to midday)

+ Degrees: 16–30 degrees Pisces

+ Totems: Bear, birch tree

+ Colours: Earth brown

✦ Crystals: Epidote

✦ Connection frequency: 8 Hz (Alpha)

✦ Transmission frequency: 144.72 Hz (D)

✦ Element: Earth

✦ Ruler: Njord (Neptune)

✦ Keywords: Regrowth, resilience, renewal

Runic compatibility

✓ With the energies of Fehu, Berkanan's resilient energy comes to the fore with grace and power. And with the energy of Isaz, Berkanan is able to endure and recover much more quickly than on its own.

✗ Berkanan and Kenaz are not so compatible, as Berkanan wants to leave the cave and Kenaz wants to go deeper into it.

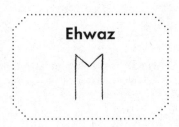

Ehwaz

✦ Dates: 20 March–4 April (from midday to midday)

✦ Degrees: 0–15 degrees Aries

+ Totems: Horse

+ Colours: Chestnut

+ Crystals: Peridot

+ Connection frequency: 4 Hz (Theta)

+ Transmission frequency: 211.44 Hz (G#)

+ Element: Water

+ Ruler: Tyr (Mars)

+ Keywords: Trust, swiftness, friends

Runic compatibility

✓ Ehwaz, the horse rune, likes to run with a herd of like-minded people. Jera and Uruz have a great relationship with it, as Jera loves to make sure things happen as they are meant to, and Ehwaz moves heaven and Earth to make them happen, while Uruz's slow, stomping moodiness is lifted by Ehwaz's excitement. Much like Eeyore and Tigger.

✗ Ehwaz does not get on well with Gebo. Ehwaz trusts implicitly and Gebo's need to demonstrate trust grates on its sensibilities.

Mannaz

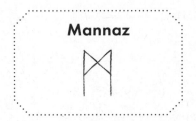

+ Dates: 4–19 April (from midday to midday)

+ Degrees: 16–30 degrees Aries

+ Totems: The human

+ Colours: Blood red

+ Crystals: Carnelian

+ Connection frequency: 9 Hz (Alpha)

+ Transmission frequency: 211.44 Hz (G#)

+ Element: Air

+ Ruler: Freya (Venus)

+ Keywords: Human spirit, human awesomeness, human resourcefulness

Runic compatibility

✓ Mannaz and Eihwaz get on well, as do Mannaz and Thurizaz. Eihwaz brings heat and contained power to the human spirit. Thurizaz brings focus and action.

✕ Mannaz and Wunjo are not the most compatible of energies. There are parts of Mannaz in Wunjo, mainly doing the work to chill out, but that's it. Mannaz likes to rush and create and manifest and do human stuff, and Wunjo is fine with that, 'Just don't do it near me, I'm chilling out.'

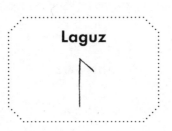

Laguz

✦ Dates: 19 April–20 May (from midday to midday)

✦ Degrees: 0–15 degrees Taurus

✦ Totems: Sea, lake, river

✦ Colours: Aqua blue

✦ Crystals: Clear quartz

✦ Connection frequency: 9 Hz (Alpha)

✦ Transmission frequency: 211.44 Hz (G#)

✦ Element: Fire

✦ Ruler: Freya (Venus)

✦ Keywords: Healing, water, washing away

Runic compatibility

✓ Laguz's healing warmth brings compassion to Ansuz and flows in and around Peroth to allow its unpredictable nature to feel nurtured.

✗ Although fairly easy-going, Laguz does not get on with Hagalaz. Combined, think Vesuvius eruption.

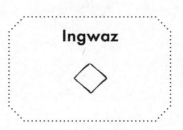

Ingwaz

✦ Dates: 5–20 May (from midday to midday)
✦ Degrees: 16–30 degrees Taurus
✦ Totems: Heroes, seed
✦ Colours: Purple
✦ Crystals: Amethyst
✦ Connection frequency: 10 Hz (Alpha)
✦ Transmission frequency: 141.27 Hz (C#)
✦ Element: Earth
✦ Ruler: Odin (Mercury)
✦ Keywords: Potential, heroic action, self-development

Runic compatibility

✓ Ingwaz works well with Raido, generating adventure-based development, and Algiz, because Algiz sets some necessary limits to Ingwaz's massive expansion.

✗ Ingwaz and Nauthiz will mire themselves in confusion, trying to grow one minute and hunkering down the next.

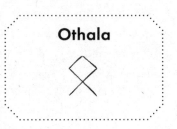

Othala

+ Dates: 20 May–5 June (from midday to midday)
+ Degrees: 0–15 degrees Gemini
+ Totems: Matriarch, home
+ Colours: Slate grey
+ Crystals: Carnelian
+ Connection frequency: 10 Hz (Alpha)
+ Transmission frequency: 141.27 Hz (C#)
+ Element: Earth
+ Ruler: Odin (Mercury)
+ Keywords: Home, castle, family

Runic compatibility

✓ Othala may feel like an Earth rune, but the watery emotions of kith and kin flow all around it like blood. It works well with Kenaz, as there will be no secrets between these two. Sowolio also gets on well with Othala. The guiding and nurturing energy of this bond makes for a strong, supportive relationship.

✗ Othala and Isaz don't gel well as Isaz is super cold, whereas Othala is like a warm cup of tea. Othala wants things to be nurturing and cosy, while Isaz likes pointed lessons and glamorous misdirection.

Dagaz

✦ Dates: 5–21 June (from midday to midday)

✦ Degrees: 16–30 degrees Gemini

✦ Totems: The day, transitions

✦ Colours: Sunset orange

✦ Crystals: Moss agate

✦ Connection frequency: 10 Hz (Alpha)

✦ Transmission frequency: 141.27 Hz (C#)

✦ Element: Air

✦ Ruler: Sunna (the Sun)

✦ Keywords: Change, transition, new beginnings, the ending of the old

Runic compatibility

✓ Tiwaz and Gebo are good companions for Dagaz. Tiwaz brings direction, honour and values to Dagaz's evolution. Gebo gives it respect and recognition as it changes state.

✗ Dagaz does not get on well with Jera. Jera likes to have measured, ordered change, while Dagaz likes all the change NOW.

Nornir runes are a path
to accessing your innate
luck and expanding your
capacity for more.

Chapter 7

Nornir Runes

This is secret and hidden lore. Or was, but now I'm telling you about it. Why not? You'd like to know how to use runic energy to get lucky, wouldn't you? And the Norns like to help you connect with your destiny, your *Orlog*. So they put energies your way to help you – Nornir runes.

Nornir runes are an energy that is unique to runic astrology. They are a hidden pathway to luck. Luck in the northern tradition is super important. As anyone who took to the iron-grey seas before the compass was invented knew, luck is life. In the frozen darkness of the ancient north, it was a powerful tool. When a cut could easily lead to sepsis and women had children young to ensure they survived childbirth, luck meant the continuation of life. When foamy-necked ships slipped into the whale road, luck would carry them home. When screaming berserkers fought each other at the behest of their king, luck would lead to victory.

Napoleon, the guy who conquered most of Europe in the early 19th century, said he'd rather have a lucky soldier than a good one.

Your Nornir rune shows how your luck manifests and how you can build it and use it most effectively. Your Nornir rune is the energy that first touched you when you emerged from your momma, right down to the very second. The Norns chose this energy to help you achieve greatness.

HOW TO FIND YOUR NORNIR RUNE

- Open up your birth chart.

- On the left of the circle, at 9 o'clock, is your rising sign, your Jord rune.

- Go to the other side of the chart, the other end of that horizon line, at 3 o'clock, and find the astrological sign and the degrees. It'll be something like 7 degrees of Aries.

- Use the 'Degrees of the Runes in the Zodiac' table (page 41) to find your Nornir rune.

HOW YOU GET LUCKY

What does this mean for you? Read on for how to take advantage of situations that you are presented with by using the runic energy the Norns have gifted to you.

Fehu

Fehu is the rune of abundance and resources. The three goddesses who spin energy into creation have spun abundance into yours. This energy is pulsing around you, ready for you to access it.

To do so, try spotting recurring patterns in your life, patterns that maybe you don't have the ability to access readily. You do have the ability to access abundance and resources by seeing these patterns and stepping into the whirl of cosmic energy that comes with them. This may be something of a stretch at first, but once you recognize the patterns and learn where the activation points are, you will be able to access all the abundance you want.

Uruz

The energy the Norns brought to your birth is that of strength and power – the strength of mental fortitude and physical power. Your gift from the Norns is to be able to bring unmatched power and strength into any situation you wish. Consciously, with grace.

In situations where nothing else is working, your strength of will, of body, mind and/or spirit will come to the fore and literally push everything else out of the way. Like the mighty aurochs, you are unassailable, immune to attack, damage or attrition. Use your strength to achieve the victory that you wish to achieve, whatever that may be, as you have the strength to make it work for you.

Thurizaz

The energy the Norns brought to your birth is that of focus and power. Thurizaz is the rune of the thunderer Thor, and when you need it, you have the power to bring yourself to a point of focus like a laser or a thorn to get what you want done. Moving towards a goal – a very specific goal – will bring you energetic fulfilment, mentally, physically and/or spiritually.

This frequency manifests in your world when you have a goal or task to work on, and will help you overcome seemingly impossible odds. Tap into it with clear goal-setting. Ignore the distractions and you will succeed, if not with grace, with a primal scream of awesome.

Ansuz

When you popped into this world, the Norns gave you the power of the voice, of communication and of the spoken word. You'll probably find that luck and fortune follow you when you trust your words and your voice. Are you expert at talking yourself into and out of situations? Does your work involve speaking? Or do you find joy in words, language and song? However you use them, words will lead you to unexpected success.

Trust your ability to talk yourself into and out of situations and use words to achieve your goals, whatever these may be. Draw on the power of communication to build your luck and enhance your experience of the world.

Raido

The moment you came into the world, the Norns blessed you with the energy of Raido, the rune of the journey, the adventure. This is where you will find luck and fortune. I'd suggest that the most awesome experiences are going to come your way when you are exploring, travelling, doing something new.

In fact, whatever you are doing, make sure there is an adventure there for you. Do you yearn to find out what happens if you press that button? That's the spirit of adventure pulsing into your life. Channel it in ways that make you feel awesome. Maybe you shouldn't press the button if there's something even better to do. Is another adventure calling you?

Kenaz

The Norns blessed you with the energy and spirit of Kenaz. Kenaz is the light in the darkness, so when everything is bleak and people are feeling down, you have the power to bring hope and light to the situation – empowering hope based on epic insight. It's built into your DNA.

Shining a light on darkness, of whatever form, may not be an obvious path to luck, but it's yours. It makes you especially powerful when working with others, as you can see the truth of a situation regardless of the confusion and darkness around you and illuminate the way forward. Which has to be good, right? Trust your ability to see things for what they really are.

Gebo

At the moment of your birth the Norns spun a web into your Runic Star Path, a web of Gebo energy, the energy of respectful giving to build relationships, alliances and co-operation.

You may well find that when the chips are down, your Nornic Runic Star Path will light up, allowing you to bring people together with respect and grace. It's in hard or stressful times that these strengths will really come to the fore, which may not sound particularly lucky, but it is in these situations where you have the power to resolve matters and achieve the victory you require. So, have confidence and draw on these diplomatic skills whenever the opportunity arises.

Wunjo

The Norns have given you the Runic Star Path of Wunjo as your helper in life, giving you the power to bring relaxation and bliss to the universe. Especially the part that you're in.

As you move through the world, you can access luck by simply allowing your Wunjo Runic Star Path to take you to the places where there are rewards for hard work. Yes, hard work, but then, for every hour you work or toil, Wunjo and the Norns will conspire to reward you with comfort and bliss. You can relax, much like a cat. In fact, 'feline' may well be how people describe you – self-assured, purring, enjoying life. How lucky is that?

Hagalaz

The Norns have decided that Hagalaz is your helper in life. They have given you the ability to take all the learning, all the gold, from a difficult situation, then burn the situation to the ground and rebuild with what you've chosen to salvage. This sounds quite drastic, but it's not. Everything in life is constantly evolving, and you're just better at it than most people.

So, lean into your ability to let entropy take its course and a bad or stale situation fall apart, then pick up the pieces. You can make your fortune from creating something new from what seems like desolation. You can even cause the desolation, if you wish.

Nauthiz

Nauthiz is need, and on the face of it need is not a pleasant sensation, it's the gasp for breath when you've been underwater too long, or the longing for a hug. Yet the Norns have spun your Runic Star Path to bring this energy to you as an asset.

In this context, Nauthiz is the ability to sense lack or need in the cosmos, including your own unconscious needs and those of others. This brings the ability to innovate, adapt and even utilize the spaces others may shy away from to ensure your needs and those of others are met. Being able to discern need is truly a gift. Use it to advantage.

Isaz

The moment you chose to pop into the world, the Norns wove the energy of Isaz into your Runic Star Path. This energy of ice, glitter and glamour is where your luck resides. When you trust what may seem ethereal or otherworldly to those around you, you may gain an unexpected victory.

The misdirection, the sleight of hand (and of mind), the 'rise above it all and skate on' energy that you have in your aura will serve you well. Your luck and fortune will grow when you lean into the confusing ways in which the world can be seen. It may be a hall of mirrors, but you will always see the truth, while others get confused.

Jera

The Norns have spun the energy of Jera into your Runic Star Path. Jera brings the harvest, and with your luck, you will get the harvest – in whatever way that energy chooses to show up.

Jera's energy will constantly attract rewards for hard work – a pay rise for showing up, a bonus for success, a client rebooking because of your good work.

The harvest can also come in the form of an internal harvest, anything from fertility to creativity. Trust your creative instincts to bring whatever project you are working on to fruition. This energy can be used communally as well. When others do what you tell them, they will reap a small portion of your harvest.

Eihwaz

Eihwaz is the yew tree – completely toxic apart from the flesh of the fruit, but able to hold a fire that will smoulder for days. So, the Norns have given you the ability to be well resourced, tough and able to withstand even the most intense heat.

You do this through filtering and controlling the energy that flows through and around you. You get to choose what energy you pick up and what you drop. If it works for you and feels good, then it's your friend. Store it until you're ready to use it. That way you have the power that is needed when it is needed. Especially useful in a crunch.

Peroth

There are two aspects to Peroth: luck and chilling with friends. The translation that I prefer is slightly more carnal. After all, what do a bunch of young men want to do after drinking and fighting all day? You get the idea, right?

When Peroth is gifted by the Norns, whenever you need to be lucky, you will be, especially if you include a sexual component, along the lines of: 'If I get this job done, I'm taking my partner out for dinner.' Luck is your friend, but don't rely on it so much that you don't do the work necessary to make things happen. When you need it, though, it will show up for you.

Algiz

The moment you popped into this world, the Norns blessed your Runic Star Path with the energy of Algiz. This brings the power to transcend borders and edges, to walk the edge of your experience, the edge of your comfort zone. This boundary-setting, edge-walking way is your lucky path. It is by being clear about where you are that you will find power and luck in your world.

The fates also conspire to bring you luck and fortune when you are clear what your 'yes' is and what your 'no' is. Being in your body, certain of where you are in time and space, will bring the victory you crave. Just don't step mindlessly over the edge.

Sowolio

The Norns wove the energy of Sowolio into your Runic Star Path as you emerged into this world. So, when a question comes up in life, don't ask your brain, as that will just give you some well-reasoned answer. Ask your heart, as that will be a better guide than anything else. This is the magic of Sowolio.

So, you'll access your luck if you go with your gut feeling, your instinct. Then Sowolio will guide you to the right choice and to the adventures that your heart and soul crave. Others may find that your ability to read situations borders on the supernatural. For you, reading paths, people and environments simply leads to fortune.

Tiwaz

The energy of Tiwaz, the rune of honour and strong values, was woven into your Runic Star Path when you were born. This energy can be relied on when the going gets tough, and you can use it to build your luck and come through those times.

Roman philosopher and statesman Cicero said, 'Esse quam videri' – always be true to yourself – and that is so true for you. Your body and spirit will always know the right course of action, so pay attention to them. When the chips are down or you are feeling unsure, trust how you feel. Your sense of honour and your values will always lead you to victory.

Berkanan

The Norns gave you the energy of Berkanan as you emerged into the world. This is the energy of birch and bear, renewal and regeneration. So, like the bear in winter, you know when to retreat and recover when your energy is low. But you're the first to reappear when the forest has burned down. The birch is the first tree to grow in scorched soil.

When life gets hard, or hectic, or overwhelming, draw on this resilient energy. Get in your cave and ride your luck while the storms of life pass you by. When they have passed, you can emerge and grow. You have the power to recover from every setback, storm or challenge.

Ehwaz

The moment you chose to pop into the world, the Norns wove the energy of Ehwaz into your Runic Star Path. Ehwaz is the companion and horse rune, so when you need luck, don't be afraid to make a friend, or to trust a friend. Or preferably several. Step into your power as a trust-builder and friend-maker. Trust others and be trustworthy yourself – dependability will draw more luck to you.

Also, use Ehwaz energy to move away from threats and hazards. A herd moves as one to find safety. You can too. It's a power move for you. You will build luck by reaching out to those you trust and moving when you need to.

Mannaz

The Norns wove the vibration of Mannaz into your Runic Star Path when you were born, and Mannaz is the energy of the human spirit, so this is where your luck and fortune lie. When life gets you down, it's time to lean into your human instincts, into the energy that has driven our species from the primordial swamp to the civilization of today.

This is a spirit of overcoming obstacles and claiming victory. In your DNA, you hold the victories of all your ancestors. When you need this vibration, it will be waiting for you. You're human, after all, aren't you? Call upon it and it will come through in every action you take.

Laguz

Laguz is the water rune, and this energy is the universal solvent – a solvent that can dissolve all toxicity and turn it, eventually, into goodness. Your Runic Star Path gives you the ability to remove the toxic energy around you to allow yourself, and others, to grow, and in your case, build your luck.

Just don't get carried away with washing the toxic away, or it will wash right back into you. Just as with dumping rubbish into the sea, if there's too much of it, it gets brought back to you on the tide. You can process it, but you may not enjoy that very much. Like having a great buffet followed by food poisoning. Unlucky.

Ingwaz

Ingwaz is the energy is of huge potential and heroic deeds. As the Norns have given it to you, draw on your potential to build your luck, especially when you need a little help in life.

Your heroic nature will come to the fore when you are under pressure. Heroism is feeling the fear and doing the thing anyway. You have this explosively epic nature. You can manifest it in dramatic Hollywood-style ways. And/or simply by growing and out-epic-ing and out-awesome-ing those who would drag you down. Know that you have the potential for heroic deeds and huge personal development built into your very energetic patterning. And you can use it however you want.

Othala

The energy that the Norns brought to your Runic Star Path at your birth is that of building community and being part of a collective. This is where your luck and fortune can be found.

Othala, the rune of the hearth and home, is the basis for this. When you are feeling secure in your home and it smells safe and feels safe, you can manifest awesome power. This applies to your community too. That community can be whatever and wherever is right for you – anything from a packed dance floor under the stars to a wooden table with a couple of friends. Just lean into it and know that the more you do, the more luck you will build.

Dagaz

The Norns have brought the energy of Dagaz to your Runic Star Path. So you can change your state – your emotions, energies, persona or physical expression – to meet the needs of a situation or access your luck. Your transformational ability will only get you so far, but your other energetic and personality traits will take you the rest of the way to victory, be that in the form of a kiss, a job, a win or a prize.

Use your shape-shifting ability to make sure that you are where you need to be and with the people you need to be with to get your needs met. And to serve your world how you want to serve.

The raw elements of creation – Fire, Earth, Water and Air – come together to form potent energies of life, magic and experience.

Chapter 8
Elemental Giants

So, we've looked at the runes and their energies. Now let's look at the other energies that flow around the cosmos and into our lives.

Here we'll look at the elements and how they interact with one another. In the northern tradition, there are four connective elements within the *Wyrd*, which is itself the fifth, the energy that binds it all together and is called *aether* in yogic circles and 'spirit' or 'the field' in metaphysical ones, and 'the force' in certain copyrighted places. These elements are primal, and if we're talking primal in the northern tradition, we're talking *Jotun*, giants.

ELEMENTS AND RUNES

The four elements are Fire, Earth, Water and Air. Each rune resonates with one of them, as follows:

Fire	Earth	Water	Air
Fehu	Uruz	Thurizaz	Ansuz
Raido	Kenaz	Gebo	Wunjo
Hagalaz	Nauthiz	Isaz	Jera
Eihwaz	Peroth	Algiz	Sowolio
Tiwaz	Berkanan	Ehwaz	Mannaz
Laguz	Ingwaz	Othala	Dagaz

Table 5: Elements and Runes

Look, I know you're going to say, 'Laguz is the water rune!' This is true. But in this context its energy is the cleansing power of Fire, the heat that comes from a healing wound.

Elemental Compatibility

The elements support or suppress one another, and sometimes cancel one another out by changing states, for example Fire and Water make steam – Water and Air.

Here's the full list:

+ Earth and Air cancel each other out.

+ Earth and Water are a powerful combination, super grounded.

+ Earth and Fire are neutral.

+ Earth and Earth are super grounding.

✦ Fire and Air expand each other. Not very grounded.

✦ Fire and Water cancel each other out.

✦ Fire and Fire can be a massive energy, or can consume each other.

✦ Air and Water work well together, but have little substance.

✦ Air and Air can go either way and are not even slightly grounded.

✦ Water and Water is the massive neap tide or a tsunami or a calm mill pond.

This is a rule of thumb, and a very broad one at that, as Laguz is fiery Water, and Kenaz is earthy Fire, and Sowolio fiery Air. There is a lot of scope to play around with this, so get to know it and make it yours.

And remember, while the gods of Asgard, the ones we see in myth and story, are relatively benevolent towards humans, the *Jotun* don't give a rat's ass. They see us as a transient annoyance. Their energy is powerful but subtle. Not like the grandeur of Odin and his one eye, or Freya and her Valkyries, more like the break in the power supply when you are trying to save your work.

Let's look at each in turn.

FIRE

In the northern tradition, the *Jotun*, the giant, who is the King of Fire, is Surtur. He lives in Muspelheim, the land of fire. Unsurprisingly.

The runic element of Fire isn't necessarily like the raging wildfire or the log fire in the camp. It *is* those things, but it's also the wildfire in the woods, the lighting strike on the pine, the cooking fire in the hearth, and the volcano spewing liquid rock into the sky. And the hammer blow of the sun in the south.

Each of the Fire runes has a different type of Fire energy:

+ Fehu: the Fire of creation

+ Raido: the Fire of adventure

+ Hagalaz: wildFire

+ Eihwaz: stored Fire

+ Tiwaz: the Fire of obligation and honour

+ Laguz: the Fire of the healing wound, the sterilization heat. And the Fire of petrol burning on water. Search for a video of it – it's scary.

All these energies interact with one another relatively well. You could say, 'They get on like a house on fire.' Have you ever been in a house fire? There's a lot of running and screaming. And a lot of heat!

EARTH

Earth energy in the north is that of rock and mountain, shore and forest, wood and peat.

Earth energy in the runes is the power of the ground beneath your feet, the rock of the mountain, the basic needs of life. If it were a chakra, it would be the root chakra. It is an energy of grounding and earthiness.

Angrboða, the Witch of the Iron Wood, is the mistress of the Earth runes.

The Earth runes are:

+ Uruz: the power and strength of the forest
+ Kenaz: the cave in the mountain
+ Nauthiz: the need and drive for life
+ Peroth: the base need for sex and luck
+ Berkanan: the energy of recovery and resilience
+ Ingwaz: the potential for growth

WATER

Water, as you might think, tends to be the antithesis of Fire, and vice versa. But in runes things aren't so straightforward. Water energies in runes are more about the movement of the energies that the runes embody and the powers that they bring from the source of life that is Water.

The Water runes, governed by Ran, the Goddess of Water, are:

✦ Thurizaz: the thunder and lightning rune

✦ Gebo: the respect rune

✦ Isaz: the ice rune

✦ Algiz: the edge rune

✦ Ehwaz: the companionship rune

✦ Othala: the hearth and home rune

AIR

The element of Air is ruled by Hræsvelgr (Hr-aes-vel-gr), a giant eagle who controls the winds that blow across the seas and mountains. His name could be translated as 'Ship-wrecker'. That gives you an idea of how he views the world.

Air is a very fast-moving element and easy to dismiss as ephemeral, but it is essential to life.

The Air runes are:

✦ Ansuz: the rune of the voice

✦ Wunjo: the rune of comfort and bliss

+ Jera: the rune of harvest

+ Sowolio: the pathway rune

+ Mannaz: the human rune

+ Dagaz: the rune of initiation and change

CONNECTIVITY

The elements are useful in looking at connectivity, either relationship-wise or in any other way, by looking at where complementary energies exist within your Runic Star Path.

Say you want to get to know someone and to know how best to do it. In classical astrology, you'd look at your birth chart to find out where your Mercury was and therefore what communication traits you had, and you'd find out where the other person's Mercury was too. Then you could see whether you were elementally compatible (see the list on page 156 for elemental compatibility). Air and Fire tend to get on well, for example – if you've ever blown on a campfire then you'll know that! Air and Earth may find it harder to ignite a spark.

In runic astrology, Mercury is Odin (more on the gods in the next chapter). So, you'd check out where he was and what sort of runic energy he was utilizing by looking at your birth chart and the 'Degrees of the Runes in the Zodiac' table (page 41).

My Odin, for example, is utilizing Hagalaz energy. So my communication style is likely to be blunt and direct. And to be honest, I kind of think it is. My wife's Odin energy is using that of Nauthiz, meaning her communication is likely to be very direct and searching for meaning.

Elementally, this is Fire and Earth energy, so not too much of a problem, relationship-wise. In terms of runic energy, these runes are close together and are both in the second *Aett*, so are on the same part of the runic pathway.

The elements aren't the only energies affecting our Runic Star Path, however. Let's look at the gods and how they rule our lives – to a greater or lesser extent, of course!

The gods, in planetary form,

have energetic magnetism.

Let them stir your soul.

Chapter 9

The Planets and Gods

Gods and goddesses are a big deal in the northern tradition. And their energies are not to be trifled with. Let's see how they affect us.

PLANETARY BODIES

Throughout time, the planets of the solar system have had names and stories associated with them, and by knowing those stories, we can see what sort of power flows around those planets. In the northern tradition, power was wielded by the gods. So, in runic astrology, the gods can represent the planets.

The gods, in planetary form, have energetic magnetism too, meaning that they are attractive to or rule (to use the astrological term) certain runes. Runic astrology hasn't gone through the mill of evolution that classical astrology has and is much less refined, so there's often a bit of an energetic tussle.

It's worth noting that in runic astrology the runes have different rulers than in 'normal' rune lore. If they work for you for all rune work, then that is right. If not, that is also right. This is your experience. Make it yours.

Also, when you've read about the gods, let them stir your soul. Get to know them. Do the rituals suggested here. Go on a voyage of discovery and find some more information about them. There are TV series, books, songs and stories out there. (I recommend the music of Wardruna.)

It's important to note that this form of discovery is an art, not a science. What you take from the stories, what you feel from the energies, is right for you. Take it all and make the meaning that feels right in your heart. Because this will be right for your work with runic astrology. The meanings you make through the experiences and events of your own life are more vital and alive than those of old, handed down through the ages.

So, let's dive into the energies, stories and resonances of the cosmos. What follows is a description of the major planetary bodies, the gods of runic astrology, and their energies and powers, which, by the way, can be illuminated by your interest. Just as when you touch your phone screen and it comes to life.

Sunna (the Sun)

Sunna is the goddess of life and light. She flows around the world (or seems to), pulling her chariot with the burning disc on it. Her light brings life and warmth, showing the way and allowing all on Earth to see the world around them.

Sunna is, however, chased by a wolf, *Sköll*, Traitor. Sköll is a very lean and tired wolf, as he doesn't stop, because Sunna doesn't stop. And he is ultimately fated to be out of luck, as the giant wolf Fenrir is destined to get to the sun before him anyway!

Sometimes, just sometimes, Sunna takes a rest, and Sköll catches her, and the light of the chariot is dimmed as the wolf grows near. But then Sunna escapes and shines her light again.

She represents the self.

Keywords

Light, life, guidance, finding your way, purpose, the self.

Colours

Yellow, white.

Energies

The way forward, guidance, navigation.

Rulership

Sunna rules Uruz, Kenaz, Sowolio and Dagaz.

Totems

Sun wheel, chariot.

Lens through which this god sees the universe

Sunna is very interested in life paths, purpose and direction. She wants the best for you and will see everything in that light. Her lens is best described as that of a kindly teacher at school who believed in you, or a favourite song that goes straight to that hidden part of you. (Mine is Starship, 'We Built This City', fyi.)

RITUAL TO SUNNA

Sunna loves to be seen, worshipped and adored. And why not? A ritual to Sunna is to get up early and greet her. This is easier in winter. Getting that first light of dawn on your face, your skin, and into your energy fields is a powerful way of expressing your gratitude to this bountiful goddess.

Manni (the Moon)

In Nordic mythology, Manni is male. A super-fluid male. Think of the most fabulous human you can think of and turn their volume up to 12. This is Manni. He travels around the cosmos in his chariot, which glows a soft luminous white.

Manni is easily distracted, and will often stop and look at things or wander off. So the wolf that chases him isn't as lean and tired as Sköll. This wolf is called *Hati*, Hate. He spends a lot of time biting Manni and his chariot. That's why Manni has lots of bites taken out of him over the course of a month and eventually gets eaten.

Manni is intuitive and mystic and is super interested in emotions and relationships.

Keywords
Emotions, feelings, intuition, sensations, psychic abilities and energy.

Colours
Pale white, neon colours.

Energies
Emotions, sensations, feelings, the metaphysical.

Rulership

Manni isn't a ruler of runes, as he's too flighty. But he has an interest in them all.

Totems

Cycles, tides, love, lust.

Lens through which this god sees the universe

Manni is a dreamer, and sees things in that way. Much like the movie *Midnight in Paris*, he always imagines the best in things and will look for the magic in any situation. As he's a mystic, he will find the magic in any situation. His world is full of goblins, wizards and trolls. He probably listens to Bowie.

RITUAL TO MANNI

As Manni is the god of emotions, connections and dreams, to ritualize your connection with him, choose a night when he's full and the sky is clear. Extra points if it's a super moon.

Go out and put yourself under Manni's gaze. If you feel comfortable, do it nude. Clothes are okay too, of course, especially if you're in a built-up area!

Feel the energy flowing from this god onto your body, into your pineal gland and through your entire system. Then go and warm up!

Odin (Mercury)

Odin is the planet closest to the sun. He is the king of the gods, and he's a warrior, magic user and rune master. He's super interested in making sure everything works. Maybe not so much legally, but practically. He's also a master orator. His words motivate millions. He loves the communication, he loves the magic. So his lens is one of communication and magic – both integral parts of leadership.

Odin regularly wanders the worlds to check that everything is going on as it should. Back in the day, this was called a progress. But remember that when the king is on his progress, either others make the decisions or you have to go and find the king to get a decision.

Odin is also a way-walker; he walks the paths of the *Wyrd* to find out what is going on in the universe. And what will be going on in the cosmos.

He chooses the most valiant dead to go to the halls of Valhalla, where they drink and fight. This keeps Odin happy, as he needs to keep an army ready for Ragnarök, the end of the world. He is a great doomsday prepper.

Keywords

Communication, leadership, magic, kingly duties, details, harmony, management, strategy.

Colours

Grey, purple.

Energies

Communication, clarity, focus, victory.

Rulership

Odin rules Ansuz, Raido, Othala and Dagaz.

Totems

Spear, raven, wolf.

Lens through which this god sees the universe

Odin is primarily interested in communication, magic, power and victory. He sees the world as a motivational seminar. Tony Robbins it and you've got Odin's lens.

RITUAL TO ODIN

Odin is the god of leadership, among many other things. A powerful ritual to him is to use his most powerful of tools: the voice.

In the shower, or on your jog, on your commute or when you walk the dog, find the time and space to sing 'Odin!' in as many different ways as you can. You can use his other names, too, such as Mr Wednesday, Grimnir, Way-walker, Furious One, or any other of his names you think fit.

Freya (Venus)

Freya is the goddess of battle, fury, beauty, feminine magic, love and lust. She also likes cats. As a goddess of magic and battle, she has very few limits on her desire to express herself and is fond of using her wit, body and magic to get her needs met.

Freya is the mistress of the Valkyries, female figures who lead the souls of the valiant dead to Valhalla – after she gets first pick for her hall. Her hall is full of beauty, love and power. The warriors there are the ones Freya wants to spend time with. It's the noisy, uncouth ones, in her eyes, that go to Valhalla.

Freya has many handmaidens who perform duties for her, anything from healing to looking after unmarried girls and uninitiated children, to birthing babies, to casting spells, to crushing the skulls of her enemies and leading her forces in battle. These handmaidens can be seen as separate from the queen of the gods, or aspects of her, depending on how you view the world. I prefer the aspects version.

Keywords
Love, beauty, joy, lust, victory, fury, cats, feminine magic.

Colours
Golden yellow, deep reds and purples.

Energies
Sex, attraction, passion, relationships.

Rulership
Freya rules Fehu, Gebo, Wunjo, Mannaz and Othala.

Totems
Valkyries, cat.

Lens through which this god sees the universe
Freya loves passion and all things passionate, such as art, love, lust and creativity. She sees the world through the lens of a Baz Luhrmann movie, all art and creativity.

RITUAL TO FREYA

Freya loves the energy of passion in any way it manifests, so a ritual to honour her is one that utilizes your passion. You can be as adult as you want here. Put passion into whatever you want to do – painting, cooking, dancing, love-making, running, practising kung fu. Whatever it is, do it with passion for the goddess of passion, love, magic and violence.

Tyr (Mars)

Tyr is the god of war, action and honour in Asgard, the home of the Norse gods. He used to be the king of the gods, but Odin took over. Probably because Odin gets people to agree, whereas Tyr shouts orders. Tyr is action-oriented and likes to think and do in the same breath. He also has firm values. His honour is unshakeable.

There's a story here. When Fenrir the great wolf was born, he was too big, and kept getting bigger, until the gods decided to chain him up, as otherwise he'd have eaten the sun. I don't know why. Maybe because the sun looks like a tennis ball and dogs like chasing tennis balls? Anyway, they chained him up with the biggest chains they could find, and Fenrir broke them. Which was annoying.

So the gods got some magic chains made out of impossible things – the roots of a mountain, the spit of a bird, the sound of a cat's footfall, the beard of a woman, the nerves of a bear and the breath of a fish. How these were forged is another story. But the gossamer-thin golden thread that was produced was used to wrap up the wolf. Who, after breaking the biggest chain in the world, wasn't going to let the gods wrap thread around him, was he? So Tyr said he'd put his right arm in the wolf's mouth, and if Fenrir couldn't break the magic chain, he could bite off the arm.

Agreed? Right.

Annnnnddddd... *unk.*

The world-ending wolf was bound safely and Tyr's arm was bitten off. Because he had given his word to the wolf and he deemed the safety of the universe to be more important than his arm. The wolf wasn't best pleased. But that's another story.

Keywords
Action, focus, war, battle, decisions, honour, values, truth.

Colours
Reds.

Energies
Action, honour, truth.

Rulership
Tyr rules Tiwaz and Ehwaz.

Totems
Chains, antlers.

Lens through which this god sees the universe
When Tyr views the universe, he sees it through the lens of doing the right thing. His view is that of the stereotypical knight in shining armour, slaying the baddies, rescuing the maidens, being true to his word. Maybe a bit like an old Schwarzenegger or Stallone movie from the eighties or nineties.

RITUAL TO TYR

The best way to honour Tyr, beyond starting a war (I think we can all agree that's a bit extreme), is to do the thing. You know the thing. You've been putting it off for ages. Procrastinating, avoiding it. Act in line with your values and beliefs and do the thing you've been putting off. Call the person, or write the letter, go to the place, have the conversation, run the marathon, join the paintball club. Whatever it is, just take action and do the thing. And do it while being mindful of Tyr.

Thor (Jupiter)

Thor is Odin's son. He has various titles, Defender of Humanity being one. He's massively strong and wields his hammer, Mjölnir, to fight off the ice giants.

Thor is, like his planet, physically bigger than the other gods. He's physically too big to walk across the Bifrost sky bridge, as he falls through it, so he gets around in a chariot pulled by two goats.

We see the Bifrost bridge, by the way, when the rain and the sun come together, especially after particularly violent thunderstorms. We call it a rainbow.

Huge himself, Thor also has huge abilities to make things bigger. He once wrestled old age and almost drank the sea dry. And dressed as a blushing bride to get his hammer back when it was 'misplaced'. But that's another story.

Thor's main role is to keep everyone safe from the giants, the elemental beings who bring fire or frost to the worlds. This is shown in astronomy as Jupiter protecting the Earth by catching or redirecting incoming asteroids.

Keywords
Big, powerful, strength, protection, expansion.

Colours
Ginger.

Energies

Protection, growth, expansion.

Rulership

Thor rules Algiz, Thurizaz and Berkanan.

Totems

Hammer, lightning.

Lens through which this god sees the universe

Thor loves protection, and food. So, he sees the universe like a German Shepherd would. Can I bite it? Is it tasty? Is it a threat?

RITUAL TO THOR

Thor isn't very picky about his rituals. He's very direct and simple. To be honest, keeping his rituals simple is definitely the way forward.

Thor likes beer, mead and food, as well as thunderstorms, so a good connecting ritual to him is, if safe during a thunderstorm, take some food and drink out for him and leave it somewhere natural, or as natural as you can.

Say, 'Mighty Thor, please accept this offering.'

If you aren't keen on being out in a storm, do it just afterwards, or wait until the planetary energy of Thor is high in the sky and do the same.

NB. Don't get struck by lightning.

Loki (Saturn)

Loki gets a bad rap. He has been demonized by Christian monks, turned from an agent of change into a monster. In truth, he's simply a god who hates being bored. So he'll actively look for ways in which things can be changed, adapted or torn down to make way for something that works better.

In the legends, Loki is completely gender and species fluid, fathering Hela, the goddess of death, Jörmungandr, the world serpent, and Fenrir, the giant wolf, while also giving birth to Sleipnir, Odin's horse. He did this while distracting a giant from building a wall.

Loki only likes structures and systems that work. If they even slightly don't work, he will set fire to them to see what happens. Whatever happens, just knowing that what comes next will be different makes it better.

Keywords

Structure, efficiency, order, challenge, change, evolution, chaos, non-binary.

Colour

Crimson.

Energies

Evolution, change, transition.

Rulership

Loki rules Jera and Eihwaz.

Totems

Fire, iron.

Lens through which this god sees the universe

Loki is super interested in what works and what doesn't work. He wants things to work. Actually, he requires things to work. On the one hand, his view is that of the old mechanic who can fix any car with a lump hammer and a socket set; on the other, he is Elon Musk on Adderall after his third espresso. Either way, he looks at the universe to see where it needs improving. And how to bring about that improvement.

RITUAL TO LOKI

Loki loves structures and systems to work. If they don't, he'll pull them down. So, a ritual to Loki is to challenge structures you feel aren't working. How? Political action, non-compliance, anything that challenges the norms of a structure that you don't agree with. You get to choose – choose the anarchy, or the structure you want to create, and do it for Loki.

These first six gods are quite interested in us as individuals. As we move out from the Earth, though, the gods get more existential in their interests and influence. They take a long time to orbit Sunna and their energy stays with each rune for a while.

So, moving on, let's have a look at these more detached energy influencers.

Urðr (Uranus)

Urðr is one of the Norns. She is the goddess of potential – she sees the potential in any situation. She loves to bring energy into being and allow her sisters to shape it. She will always act in what she sees as the best way, but she has very little compassion. Because she handles the energy of trillions, she doesn't really care about one individual, but if you make an interesting case, well... that's different.

Keywords
Fate, chance, potential, destiny, purpose.

Colours
Deep blues and purples.

Energies
Fate, potential, destiny, purpose.

Rulership
Urðr rules Peroth.

Totems
Womb, dice cup.

Lens through which this god sees the universe
Urðr has something of a soft-focus view of the universe, being drawn to energies that sparkle. Think of her gaze as that of a toddler in a toy shop. She will always be drawn to the next shiny thing, while spinning tens of trillions of threads into a complex tapestry of life. Her gaze is soft and all-seeing, but will only focus on something if it's interesting to her.

RITUAL TO URÐR

A ritual to honour Urðr is one that recognizes her weaving of the threads of fate into the *Wyrd*. This one requires some energy and focus from you: spin or weave or knit something.

Spin fleece into thread, weave thread into cloth, or knit yarn into cloth. Or, if that isn't for you, 'man knitting' paracord can work too. Choose bright, bold colours.

Njord (Neptune)

Njord is the Nordic god of the sea, of its unknown depths and hidden mysteries. He follows the tides of fate and mystery, discovering hidden treasure or resources, while with the other hand dragging you down into inky darkness. He's interested in what lies beneath, in dreams and altered states, and in hypnotic energy, mind control, glamour, magic and the depths of the soul.

Keywords

Dreams, depths, altered states, walking between worlds, between universes.

Colour

Deep sea greens and blues, and darkness as the absence of light.

Energies

Dreams, shamanic journeys, altered states.

Rulership

Njord rules Isaz and Laguz.

Totems

Boat, fishing net.

Lens through which this god sees the universe

Njord sees the universe as a dream, kind of like the movie *Moulin Rouge*, when everyone has drunk absinthe. The connections and correlations are weird, wonderful, and work. Njord loves the dreamy energy that comes from the imagination and depths of creativity. But you've got to get super Dali-like to get his attention.

RITUAL TO NJORD

Njord is the lord of the seas, rivers and lakes, and loves sparkling copper. So, making an offering of chocolate (biodegradable) 'copper' coins to waters is a powerful way of getting his blessing. Take the wrapping off first. The wilder the water, the more powerful the blessings. Be sensible, though – a Force 9 hurricane is not the place to seek blessings!

Myrmir (Pluto)

Myrmir is a *Jotun*, a giant. He lives in a deep, dark, icy pool. And he's a disembodied head. Which makes it hard to get out and about. Because of this, Myrmir keeps himself occupied by harvesting the universe's wisdom. Anything that could be even slightly useful finds its way into the vast memory of this bobbing head. Ever bobbed for apples? Myrmir is the apple.

Odin went to Myrmir to find the secrets of the runes. And that wisdom cost him an eye – an eye that now bobs next to Myrmir in his dark well.

Myrmir holds all the potential wisdom and power of the universe. But can't do anything about it. So he manipulates others to get his needs met.

Keywords

Wisdom, knowledge, power, learning, sarcasm, development, manipulation.

Colours

You know the colour of freshly hewn icebergs? That dark blue is Myrmir's colour.

Energies

Wisdom, power, manipulation.

Rulership

Myrmir longs for power, and his runes, Hagalaz and Nauthiz, help it flow his way.

Totems

Scrying mirror, well.

Lens through which this god sees the universe

Myrmir sees the universe as one of those sleazy pick-up artist seminars – it's all about having power over others and getting his needs met. This lens may not be a pleasant one, but it is effective.

RITUAL TO MYRMIR

Myrmir is notorious for asking for weird things in his rituals. Odin had to sacrifice an eye. *Do not cut out your eye.* Use a mirror for your ritual, or a scrying stone if you have one. Or you can use a well, or other pool of water.

Slow your breath and gaze at your reflection. Ask for Myrmir's blessing. He'll probably send you weird dreams if he does take an interest in you.

Mengloth (Chiron)

Mengloth is a *Jotun*, of the same clan as Myrmir but with very different interests. Her home is a mountain in the heart of the icy wastes. Within said mountain are many rooms, each with a special function.

These are not *Fifty Shades*-type rooms. They are healing rooms – saunas, apothecary shops, birthing chambers, rooms of dying, rooms of bone-setting, rooms of any other form of healing you can think of. And Mengloth's doors are open to all. She is a healer in the purest sense of the word. She has many acolytes who go out into the universe and heal. But she is the original and best.

Keywords

Healing in all its forms.

Colour

Infra-red.

Energies

Healing – spiritual healing, physical healing, mental healing, diagnostic healing.

Rulership

Mengloth does not rule any runes.

Totems

Geothermal pool, ice plunge pool.

Lens through which this god sees the universe

Mengloth is the ultimate healer. She looks at the universe with an eye to heal and help. She views everyone as a patient and will provide healing whenever she is asked.

RITUAL TO MENGLOTH

Mengloth loves healing. And she is super practical. So, a powerful ritual to her would be to do a first-aid course or community CPR course. Do this mindfully and she is likely to pay you some attention.

WORKING WITH THE GODS' ENERGY

Right, we've had a look at how the gods view the universe and what they are interested in. With that information, we can begin to work out how they will influence the energies flowing around them.

When cosmic energy flows past these cosmic entities, it gets manipulated by their gravitational pull. Just as light shines through raindrops and splits to form a rainbow, so energy flows around the planets and splits. This energy then lands on the Earth in frequencies and wavelengths that affect us in very subtle ways.

Looking at the energy distortion that comes through the lens of each planet, we can see where that affects the world, and the runes and us. The fact that the gods' energy impacts us at birth means that it influences our cells. And as such, how we develop. And not just us – everything.

Let's look at how we can use this.

This is how we can use runic astrology to connect to the deeper powers of the universe to see when and how to act to achieve our goals and find victory.

For example, my last book, *Runes Made Easy*, came out on 30 November 2021. The gods interested in books are Odin and Loki – Odin from the communication, magic and runes angle, and Loki in terms of structure and time-scale. Where were they in the cosmos at that time?

Odin brought his energy to my book launch in Algiz, and Loki brought Gebo energy. So I could see that the launch would be guarded and limited from a communications perspective, but the book's reputation would grow over time. Loki likes time. This has proven to be accurate. *Runes Made Easy* had a guarded launch, but has gained in energy as time has gone on.

Would you like to look at the cosmos and see how that might affect your own life?

CONSULTING THE GODS

Choose an upcoming event in your life – a new job maybe, or first date.

Plug that date into your astrology app and see where the planets will be then.

Go through and translate this information into the runic energies (see 'Degrees of the Runes in the Zodiac' table, page 41). The fact you have to do it manually will build those Runic Star Path energies into you.

What type of energy do you need? Will you be having an interview or giving a presentation? If so, see what runic energy Odin holds on that date.

What about love? What's the best way to impress that special person? See where Freya is and if there are any gods bringing Peroth energy.

Being able to see where the energy you require is present in the cosmos is a powerful tool. And sometimes an energy is worth waiting for.

PLANNING AHEAD

You know what you'd like to do and the result you'd like to get. You've worked out what sort of energy would suit your needs. So all you need now is a little patience, because you might not need to do anything now, for the best may be yet to come.

You may, for example, just take a look at the cosmos and go, 'Ooh, in two years' time the beginning of June is going to be epic for moving house. And this December is going to be the best time for us to get married, as Freya will be in Othala.'

Patience and planning can bring a host of power and victory to your world. This is how the gods do things.

When the gods wander,
their attention drifts.
The energies they
rule can go awry.

Chapter 10

Wandering Gods

In classical astrology there is a concept called retrograde. This is when a planet or astral body appears, from our perspective on Earth, to go backwards in the sky.

In runic astrology, what this does is move the energy of a god away from their domain. The gods can find that sitting on the throne all the time is tiring, so they get up sometimes and have a look around. Wander off. Leave their responsibilities behind. When Odin (Mercury) wanders, for example, communication gets squiffy. Professional word, squiffy.

There is another way of looking at a wandering god. The planets aren't physically going backwards, our view of them is. So this means that this time of wandering is a time of reassessing and revisiting the energies that come from that god. It's a time of reflection.

Let's look at the gods in turn and what their wandering means for us.

Sunna (the Sun)

Sunna does not wander. She is the heart of the solar system and all life flows from her and the other gods dance for her. She does sometimes get eclipsed, though. When she is, her energies of life and creation, path-setting and purpose, stop. Kind of like the reset button on the computer. When she comes back, though, there is fresh energy to utilize. The old can be dropped. You don't have to open the proverbial browser with all the tabs on it, just open a new window on life.

Manni (the Moon)

Manni does not wander but, like Sunna, he does get eclipsed, and he has a cycle of being full and then having chunks bitten out of him by the wolf Hati, who bites him to get him to keep moving, until he is finally eaten altogether and then has to regrow to become full again.

The fuller Manni is, the more influence he has. And when he is eclipsed, about once every 18 months, his energy is reversed. So check where his influence is when the eclipse is happening.

Odin (Mercury)

Odin wanders around the skies regularly, and when he does, his interests get left on the table. So energies around communications lose any oversight and can go haywire.

This happens about three times a year for about a month.

Freya (Venus)

Freya is primarily interested in keeping house, raising children and being the queen of slaughter and magic. So when she wanders, you may find that passion, friendships, relationships and home life gets confusing, or that things you've previously ignored in those areas come and bite you on the bum.

What's different and interesting about Freya's wandering is that she doesn't *just* go backwards, she also goes behind the sun for a while and is no longer visible in the sky. She begins her cycle as the morning star for approximately seven months, disappears into the darkness for about 40 days and returns as the evening star for roughly seven months. (Lisa Lister talks more about this in her book *Self Source-ery*.)

In Norse mythology, the darkness is where the *Draegr*, the dwarves, live, in the caves below the mountains and volcanos. The *Draegr* are the best weapon smiths, armour smiths and craftspeople. If you want bling, go to them. They also host a mean party.

So, Freya goes into the darkness to have fun, get the best bling and reinvent herself. Whereas the other gods go exploring when they wander, Freya gets drunk, has fun, goes to the spa and goes shopping. She returns refreshed and renewed as a wild warrior.

Freya wanders every 18 months, for about 43 days.

Tyr (Mars)

When Tyr goes wandering, decisive action, honour, values and beliefs are left unattended, which may result in poor decisions and actions and a lot of blundering into situations without checking them out effectively. Be especially aware of energy around promises at this time. They can be misjudged easily.

Tyr goes wandering every 26 months. And this meander around the cosmos lasts eight to 10 weeks.

Thor (Jupiter)

When Thor gets bored and wanders off, because he is too big for the rainbow bridge, he falls through it, and his energy sinks deep, and growth, expansion and safety may feel less grounded and life feel a little more trying. Remember Thor is a first-line defence only, and he expects you to look after yourself for the most part. Imagine a guard dog full of sausages. He is there, but getting him to move is hard.

Thor wanders every year for about four months.

Loki (Saturn)

Loki likes to party like a college kid in Ibiza, and when he wanders, he doesn't so much drop his interests as slam-dunk them, and doesn't even bother with an out-of-office. If it won't keep going without him watching over it, why should he bother with it anyway? So, during this time structures and standards that you may hold dear may well show cracks. Pay attention to those cracks. As where they are is where you can grow.

Loki wanders for about four and a half months a year.

Urðr (Uranus)

When this Norn wanders, relying on your 'fates' to sort you out may not be the best idea. What you'd planned to do may well get a little confused. Urðr's energy is much more etheric than that of the previous gods, and much more subtle. But when she gets back, she'll definitely pick up the reins again.

Urðr spins off on adventures for about five months of the year.

Njord (Neptune)

Njord is even further away from Earth than Urðr, so his domain of altered states and untapped depths needs less control. When he gets bored and wanders off, though, you may find that connection to the unconscious is less stable, or indeed more solid, depending on your personal energy codes.

Njord wanders off every six months or so.

Myrmir (Pluto)

Let me start this with the fact that Myrmir doesn't give a toss. He lives in a well in the bottom of a cave and will quite happily ignore the universe to bask in his own awesomeness. He is a disembodied head, after all.

He can't wander, but he does sulk and spend time deliberately ignoring everything and everyone, and then his hold over the innate subtle powers of development, deep learning and hidden wisdom is less firm. And thus they are harder to find. Not that it's easy in the first place. But Myrmir kind of likes the idea that the search for self-knowledge should be a challenge.

Myrmir goes wandering for six months a year. Less wandering, more turning his face and bobbing away, content to keep his knowledge and wisdom to himself.

Mengloth (Chiron)

When the cosmic healer goes wandering, this is more like a doctor stuffing a sandwich at the nurses' station than a sabbatical. The other parts of the team are still functioning, but healing isn't quite as efficient during this time, because the expert is enjoying a cup of bad coffee and a slightly stale sandwich. Expect that your energetic healing experiences will require a little more effort. Perhaps more crystals and more sacred smoke.

Mengloth goes retrograde for about five months of the year.

From the runic to the cosmic, Yggdrasil, the world tree, is the source of the energies that flow into us.

Chapter 11

The World Tree

Yggdrasil, the world tree, or Milky Way as you may know it, stretches across the night sky, its branches reaching glimmering into the infinite darkness and casting energetic shadows that have a profound influence on those below.

From the runic to the cosmic, Yggdrasil is the source of the energies that flow into us. Over billions of miles, these energies flow towards us, to help us be as powerful as possible.

Within classical astrology there is the concept of houses – twelve 30-degree segments of the chart wheel that run counter-clockwise from the rising sign. Each house has a theme, which provides context for the signs and gods/planets within that house.

In runic astrology, the house system comes from Yggdrasil's branches, *Stamme*, stretching across the heavens and casting shade in which the gods and runes rest. This system came to me straight from the *Wyrd*.

Like the houses, the *Stamme* run anti-clockwise from your rising sign, your Jord rune, on your birth chart, changing every 30 degrees. In fact, they map onto the houses that a classical natal or other astrology chart would give you – you can find them both on the outer rim of the chart, numbered one to twelve – but the energies are different. What are they?

As well as an outline of each *Stamme*, I'll give you the runic energies that resonate with each one. These runes are more powerful when found in this *Stamme* on your Runic Star Path/birth chart.

Also listed is the god whose energy works well with that particular *Stamme*. Their energy is magnified when they are found there.

First *Stamme*: Mod (Moad)

 Mod is the branch of emotions and feelings. Its energy is that of the internal self. Emotions, feelings, self-belief, drive, values and beliefs all reside here.

Having a god in this *Stamme* means the energies of that god are swayed towards the internal emotions, feelings, ego and self.

✦ Runic energies: Ehwaz and Mannaz

✦ God energies: Tyr

Second *Stamme*: Litch (Leech)

Litch is the branch of the physical – the body, the physical connection to the world. It's about the potential held within our cells and how we act in the world.

Having a god in this *Stamme* leads the energies of that god towards our physical experiences of life, from our body and health to how we interact with the physical world.

✦ Runic energies: Laguz and Ingwaz

✦ God energies: Freya

Third *Stamme*: Vili (Vi-li)

Vili is the branch of the will – the inner energy, force and power that motivates us, pushes us through hard times and allows us to survive and excel. Odin has a brother named after this power.

Having a god here lends the resonance of that god to our will-power, our drive, business ventures, conquests and victories.

✦ Runic energies: Othala and Dagaz

✦ God energies: Odin

Fourth *Stamme*: Kinfylgja (Kin-feel-gh-yah)

 Kinfylgja is the branch of ancestry, the energy of our forebears – our ancestors of blood, bone and spirit:

+ Ancestors of blood are those who have the same blood as us, or have taken us into their blood – usually immediate family and close friends.

+ Ancestors of bone are those who are long dead, who are bones. For example, those who fell in the Great War, or took dangerous journeys across the seas to a new world and a new life. Those who fell stopping those invaders.

+ Ancestors of spirit are those who inspire us with their deeds – artists, warriors, leaders, lovers, mothers. These spirits can have existed in the real world or be mythic energies. They are equally powerful.

So, this *Stamme* holds the magic of the spiritual wisdom that flows through our DNA, our blood, and the wisdom that sings in our soul from a story or movie.

Having a god in this *Stamme* brings that energy to our experience of family, ancestry, past lives, friendships and relationships. As well as sex, dating and pets.

+ Runic energies: Fehu and Uruz

+ God energies: Manni

Fifth *Stamme*: Æthem (Ahh-th-em)

 Æthem is the branch of magic and creativity. *Æthem* means 'power' or 'energy' in Old English. This energy is that of creation, inspiration and joy.

Magic lies in this *Stamme*, as do inspiration and personal power. Anything that stimulates, motivates or encourages our growth in the world resides here. A god, if present, brings their influence to that creative aspect of life.

✦ Runic energies: Thurizaz and Ansuz

✦ God energies: Sunna

Sixth *Stamme*: Litr (Leet-r)

Litr is the branch of health, of life energy. This energy is more than just good health, it's the ability to bring the experience of life to bear. To be resilient, supple and soft. To be adaptable, strong and powerful. Eastern traditions call this energy *kundalini*.

The energies affecting our health and experience of health in the world are held in this *Stamme*. While Litch controls the physical, Litr brings the energy of, well, energy to our experience. From an Eastern viewpoint, this is chakra energy, or *chi*, or *prana*. *Ond* in Nordic terms. Shamanic power and other energies like this live here, and any gods who are present influence how our energy flows.

✦ Runic energies: Raido and Kenaz

✦ God energies: Odin

Seventh *Stamme*: Gothi (Go-thee)

Gothi is the branch of connectiveness. A Gothi is a holy person, a higher self. Picture this energy as the roots of a tree, linked to all the relationships you have in your life – not just in terms of sex and intimacy, but work, life, dogs and that goose that cackles at you in the park.

This *Stamme* also brings the energy of our higher self, of how we connect to the spiritual powers of the universe, of the spiritual connections we build. Our spiritual life-partner energy lives here – this is where we can look to get insights into how to find our life partner.

✦ Runic energies: Gebo and Wunjo

✦ God energies: Freya

Eighth *Stamme*: Maegen (Maah-gen)

Maegen is the branch of the actions that elevate us in the world. Not external experiences, more personal evolution. This *Stamme* has great power to direct the course of our life. And to surprise us in ways we may not expect. The energies here show us how to mitigate those surprises.

The gods within this *Stamme* show us the path to self-development – where we can excel and what energies we'd benefit from cultivating to improve ourselves.

✦ Runic energies: Hagalaz and Nauthiz

✦ God energies: Myrmir

Ninth *Stamme*: Orlog (Or-lag-gh)

Orlog is the branch of personal destiny. Not to be confused with the *Wyrd*. These energies are sisters, not the same. Orlog is our path through life. This energy helps us access spirituality and make a connection to the divine.

This life-path energy is influenced by the gods that reside in this *Stamme*. The experiences we encounter will be amplified if we look at them through the lenses of these gods.

✦ Runic energies: Isaz and Jera

✦ God energies: Thor

Tenth *Stamme*: Hamingja (Hai-ming-ya)

Hamingja is the branch that holds the reputation and luck we experience in life. This *Stamme* helps us plot a course through life by showing us where we will excel and find our victory.

The gods that reside here will help us discover our path to luck, our *karma* if you will. Look to the little choices in life that can lead you down the path of victory and make them with these gods in mind.

✦ Runic energies: Eihwaz and Peroth

✦ God energies: Loki

Eleventh *Stamme*: Fylgja (Feel-gyah)

 Fylgja is the branch of our connection to spirit, the divine and the gods. It shows us the practical and spiritual path to follow to make that connection. *Fylgja* is the Old Norse for 'spirit guides'.

This *Stamme* holds the energy of our spirit guides, angels, ancestors – any spirits that we can connect with in order to be in communion with the divine and other realms.

✦ Runic energies: Algiz and Sowolio

✦ God energies: Urðr

Twelfth *Stamme*: Ve (Vay)

Ve is the branch of the hidden or mystic parts of life – the occult, the forbidden, the hidden motivations, the fetishes, all that is unspoken and concealed. All of that is here, ready to be known. Psychic, prophetic and other forgotten abilities are here too.

This is the *Stamme* of the darkness in our soul, and the path through that darkness and fear. But we don't have to take it.

✦ Runic energies: Tiwaz and Berkanan

✦ God energies: Myrmir

CONNECTING WITH YOUR *STAMME*

The *Stamme* of your Runic Star Path show you how to navigate your life and deepen your experience of it.

- Right now, get your natal chart and check where the houses are (on the outside of the chart). Usefully, as mentioned earlier, *Stamme* and houses map onto each other, so now you know where your *Stamme* are too.

- Look at the chart and find your Sunna rune. See what *Stamme* your Sunna is in.

- What energies, frequencies and vibrations are coming from the world tree with your Sunna rune? Feel into that energy.

- When you feel called, feel into the other planets and build your understanding of your Runic Star Path.

Can you see, and more importantly feel, how the energies of the runes and the gods interact to form your Runic Star Path?

Chapter 12

Connections

We've come a long way. We've reached so far. Now it's time to bring all this information together to see, and more importantly feel, how the energies of the runes and the gods interact to form Runic Star Paths.

In Norse mythology, cosmic interactions are likely to be expressed in the form of arguments, make-ups, break-ups, stupid pranks and consuming too much ale. Ours is a different world, with different stories, but still the interactions between cosmic bodies create energetic waves, connections and distortions that affect us in different ways. So let's have a look at these energy patterns.

What happens, for instance, when the gods form aspects to one another? First of all, I'm going to look at five of these aspects, the major ones.

THE MAJOR ASPECTS

As you know, runic astrology works alongside classical astrology. 'Aspects' is a term from classical astrology. It describes the patterns that are formed when gods/planets are in certain places around us, and the vibrations that follow on from energy being shaped by those patterns. They've been formalized in classical astrology, and they work. So I'm not going to mess with them.

What I'm going to do is use planet names to describe the celestial bodies being plotted here, but of course you can think of these energies in terms of Norse gods if you wish.

Let's look at the five major energetic interactions.

The Conjunction

This is when two planets are so close to each other they are in the same runic energy. For example, if Mars (Tyr) and Mercury (Odin) are both at 0 degrees of Libra, they will be 'conjunct in Kenaz'. Looking at a chart where planets are conjunct, you'll see two planetary symbols with the same zodiac symbol and the same or a very close number in brackets.

A conjunction means that the planets' energies are united. They are working together. Perhaps at a party, perhaps in battle, or perhaps just putting IKEA furniture together. Whatever it is, their energies are pulling in the same direction, working together for success. The closer they are in degrees, the more powerful their joint energy.

The Sextile

This is when two planets are 60 degrees apart from each other. In this formation, their combined energy makes a triangle, which causes the energies to combine to work towards the same goal. This is more likely to be throwing a party than starting a war, as there will probably be drinks involved. But not too many – the sextile shows the *intelligent* use of the combined power.

The Square

Here, the two planets are 90 degrees apart. This formation sees them at opposite ends of an energy, creating tension. Think series finale of *Housewives of Asgard*. Or being drunk at 1 a.m. outside a sleazy pub and not talking properly. Heading to the kebab shop, but not really caring any more. Probably losing a shoe. 'And who's got my phone? Really? And why is there sick in my bag?'

With this energy, you'll get there. It probably won't be fun. But what good story ever started with 'We were drinking tea'? (Okay, as mentioned earlier, *The Hobbit* came close.)

The Trine

This is when the planets are 120 degrees apart and making a very strong triangle. Remember maths at school? Trigonometry? Remember triangles are the strongest shape for load-bearing? Planets in trine support each other.

This energy makes for super-strong alliances, so it's a beneficial frequency to use to get stuff done.

The Opposition

Here the planets are opposite each other. In opposition. They are 180 degrees apart on a chart. Think of this energy as two sides of a bargaining table, or a tug-of-war. Both sides are right, and they are both trying to win.

The real win here is to make sure you take a breath and try to see things from the other side, or it's going to get messy.

Fuzziness

Because we're humans, not computers, I always allow some 'calculation' error in looking at aspects, usually one to five degrees. This gives me chance to catch the fast-moving celestial bodies like Mercury, Venus, the Moon and the Sun.

You can be as draconian as you like with your readings, but remember the difference in a degree of movement for Mercury can be less than a day. So if you are doing a runic astrology reading in New York for someone in London, there may be different degrees in play because of time zones. Just something to bear in mind if you ever become a professional runic astrologer. Studying the Runic Star Paths of others, like the dog, your partner, your friends, or even paying clients, is a way of getting a deeper understanding of the runic influences on their lives, and so coming to understand the runic influences on us all.

THEN VS NOW

Or for you astro-geeks, natal chart transits

The gods/planets don't just make connections in the here and now, they also make connections with the then – the moment you were born, and the gods/planets of your natal chart. Your natal chart, you'll remember, is the term traditional astrology uses to refer to your birth chart, or in my terms, your Runic Star Path.

In traditional astrology, these connections are called transits, because the god/planet is transiting through the cosmos. I'm going to use that word too.

Transiting Gods

Throughout the myths and stories of the ancient north, the gods fall out, make friends, play pranks on one another and generally get on or don't get on. That's how gods work. And, as we've already seen, each god has interests and influences, and sometimes they align, others not so much.

The way to work out if the gods are friends at the moment is to look at where they are now. What patterns are they making?

As you now know, as a (very) broad rule of thumb, if two gods are conjunct, they're on the same page; if sextile, they're getting ready for a party; if trine, there's a strong supportive energy between them; if in opposition, it's time to grab your sword!

We can also look at the rulers of the runes and the mythology of the northern tradition to find out if the gods are getting on. Some gods have obvious alliances. Freya and Odin get on well, as they are married. Freya and Loki, however, tend to get annoyed with each other quite quickly, as Loki likes to play pranks and Freya likes slightly more adult humour.

Looking at what the gods are up to now can be compared to getting an overall weather forecast, but let's get personal. Comparing what's happening now to what was happening at the moment of your birth will show how your personal energies are being affected by the current now of the cosmos.

For example, what is your Sunna rune? Let's use my wife's, Hagalaz. As I write this, Sunna has energy from Laguz. Going back to Chapter 6, where we looked at runic compatibility, we can see that Laguz and Hagalaz aren't the best of friends and they don't mix well. So there is potential for energies to combust here. As Sunna shows the way, and Hagalaz and Laguz are causing problems and explosions, there is the potential for Lisa's way ahead to be a bit 'choppy'. She'll need to take care not to be thrown off course.

Remember when I talked about lenses of energy? Well, think of your natal chart as a light source and the current transits as the lenses through which you see said light. Like looking at the sun through a stained-glass window in a church. You are the sun. Isn't that nice?

So, if, for example, you've got Freya in Fehu on your Runic Star Path and transiting Freya is in Gebo, then you've got to look at the abundance of passion and love through the gifts and respect of that passion.

We can also apply the above aspects to this interaction. To take another example, say Freya in Gebo is conjunct your natal Freya (there are some astro words for you), meaning that these energies are both present for you. That's just going to amp up that power, making the frequency of that energy even more potent for you.

On a practical note, when you look at current transits vs the positions of the planets/gods on a natal chart, the picture your app will usually give you is one that has your birth chart in the middle of some circles, like the hub of a wheel, and the current energies are on the outer ring. Your app may well do it differently. Have a play.

The important takeaway from looking at current transits vs your natal chart is that you can look at how the energies of a specific date affect your personal energy. Isn't that useful? Which brings us to our final chapter....

The pulse of cosmic runic
energy that touches
our planet has subtle
and profound effects.

Chapter 13

Using Runic Resonance

Now we're going to get practical. Because I like things to be useful and I want you to be able to use what I share here in a really tangible way to understand yourself better, know why you do the things you do and work with the energetics of the cosmos to navigate the seas of the current times.

We've touched on this along the way, but now we're going to look more closely at how to use the powerful energies that you have come to know are part of your life. This is the point of runic astrology: to understand and utilize the patterns and processes of the universe to create the experience we crave and long for. To work with the energies that are happening anyway to find joy, love, success and victory.

This isn't to say that you are bound by the paths in the stars. Far from it. Runic astrology shows us the paths we *can* take.

It provides navigational aids to help us through the confusion – aids we can choose to access or not. Kind of like how bears can take advantage of the spawning time to go and eat salmon.

Be the bear, not the salmon.

UNDERSTANDING

Of course you've got to know where you are before you can go anywhere, or start to tweak the threads of the *Wyrd* to create what you'd like to see in your life.

Runic astrology can give us a greater understanding of where we are and how we are. From our birth chart, we can come to understand our strengths and weaknesses and the energies we have to work with, and how we can work with other people. For example, you might be wondering, 'If I go on a date with this person, will it work?' or 'My team-mate is this Sunna rune, will our energies work well together?'

To work out whether you are compatible with someone, look to where there are complementary energies in the runes in your charts. For instance, my wife and I have the same Mengloth energy, similar Odin energy and complementary Sunna energy.

What if you're working with someone and want to know about their ability to manage change? Where is their Loki energy?

What if you have your eye on them and are wondering about their style of love, romance and magic? Where is their Freya energy?

Say, for example, you're looking for love. Where can you find it? This is a common question.

To find out where love (or anything else) might be for you, you need to translate your thinking into the language of the Norns and the cosmos. Try it now.

WHAT IS LOVE IN RUNIC LANGUAGE?

First of all, ask yourself what love means to you. Is it honour perhaps? Adventure? Sex? Family?

Check the table of runes starting on page 4. See which runic associations marry with your ideas.

Now look to where those energies are on your Runic Star Path.

Remember to look for the gods too, and see where they are, which Stamme they are influencing.

Your next question may be: 'When am I going to find love?' Which brings us to...

DIVINATION AND TIMING

One of the things people are desperate for is insight and wisdom in regard to a situation, or how the future is going to pan out. We love to meaning-make, we rarely like to be surprised and we love to know *why*.

What does a toddler ask? 'Why? Why? Why?'

Astrology is able to provide a why. And a when. And a 'yes' or 'no'. From 'When will I find my one?' to 'Will I get promoted?' to 'Shall I write that book?' You know the questions that you'd like to ask the fates, right? Well, it's possible that *all* the answers are to be found in your natal chart.

What astrology is good at is spotting the energies that will be experienced through the frequencies of the waves that hit the Earth at any given time, depending on the planetary alignments. And what makes it accessible is that it's an art married with science, relying as much on creativity as on a calculator.

Astronomy is the science bit. Astronomy tells us where the planets and moons and asteroids will be. They follow predictable courses. People in dark rooms with big telescopes spend their whole careers looking at the night sky to discover new things and to study the paths that we *think* we know.

Astrology is the art of said science. The predictability of planetary movement means that we know that when the sun is in one place, and the moon in another, and the constellation of Libra is in another place, the energies that affect our world are the same, or roughly the same, as they were when this happened last year, or last decade, or last century, or last millennium.

The art of astrology helps us know that people with a Libra Sun sign have similar tendencies. Or that Leo people are gregarious. And we know that those specific energies will be present at certain times in the cyclical calendar of planetary alignments. This extends past people into events.

Look at big collective events such as the coronation of King Charles in the UK, or the timing of elections or invasions. The people who are making the decisions may well be basing them on the cosmic energies. We know the British royal family has used astrologers for centuries, and that titans of industry use astrology too, as do politicians and warlords. Why? Because it works.

Another example of this is the Super Bowl. The dates, start times and location of this great sporting event all change. Why? Why not have a national stadium or standard date? Or any other standardization? Because the cosmic energies hitting the stadium at the time influence results, sales and the collective ritual that is 100 million people focusing on one event. Powerful stuff.

Due to the predictable nature of the cosmos, we know where planets, moons and asteroids are going to be on any specific date. Using maths that is more complex than my brain can cope with (I checked), we can find out where the energy of the cosmos is flowing and when and how. For any date, past, present or future, anywhere in the world.

So, perhaps you want to write a book. You can look at when the planets will be most supportive to writing that book. Where are the planets now? Are they harmoniously aligned or not? What transits are affecting you personally? What will it be like next week?

I work this out by looking at an astrology chart that an app or program has given me. I know proper astrologers do this with a protractor and calculator. My friend David Wells is a master at this (give him a Google). I'm not, so I use tech. Modern Viking, me.

What date will the energies of the cosmos be good for my book to be well received? When should I send my proposal to the editor, knowing that there are cosmic energies that will help me get the result I need and want?

This is how we can divine with astrology: we look at known energy points, known book publishing success for example, and use that known space to find where and when the cosmological energies will be similar again.

Would you like to know how to find two or more energy points that you can use to work out how to get your needs met within the *Wyrd* of the cosmos?

Using Your Runic Star Path for Divination

Each god has influence over at least two and often more runes (see Chapter 9). Freya, for example, has influence over Fehu, Gebo, Wunjo, Mannaz and Othala. This means that when any of those runes in your Runic Star Path are being influenced by Freya, by being in a positive aspect to her, you'll have a better chance of finding the love you want.

Now let's get epic. If you have any of those runes (Kenaz, Gebo, Wunjo, Mannaz, Laguz and Ingwaz) in your Runic Star Path, then Freya has influence over that aspect of your energetic being.

Look to where your Sunna rune ruler and Freya are in relationship. Perhaps your Sunna rune is Ansuz, you great speaker, you, and Odin and Freya are conjunct on the chart. This means that there is the potential for relationship or love energy to come through your language skills and Odin's leadership and Freya's passion.

With three points like this, you can have a very clear direction to go in. You know you must act with your voice, leadership and passion. So, take the first step. Speak to the person. Ask them out. Perhaps send them a text. With those three energetic influences to navigate by, you can find a clear Runic Star Path for your lovin'.

The same is true for all aspects of life – health, wealth, pets, book launches, starting a new job. Use the same process:

✦ Find the energies you want.

✦ Find the ruler of those energies.

✦ Using your app, look to where those points come together in a beneficial relationship.

Want to get a promotion? Loki in Fehu may be good, but Loki in Fehu and Sunna in Hagalaz will shake stuff up when they are square, and that might be good for your prospects too.

Say you've met a hot human in a café. Knowing their Sunna rune will help you realize where their energetic influences are. Perhaps they are a Nauthiz Sunna, so Thor is their ruler. From that you know that when Thor is in your own energies, or your energies are being influenced by Thor, super-direct action to get the relationship moving will be effective. And as Nauthiz is their Sunna rune, well, they will appreciate direct action and communication.

Choosing the right energy for your decision, event, proposal, job interview or kiss is important. There's plenty of energy to choose for your event. Look at how the transits of a specific time affect you. Be specific. If you want healing energy, look to Mengloth, or planets in Laguz. If you want shamanic energy, look to Odin. He's useful for communication as well. And Mannaz has that vibe too, while Tyr has action and honour. So does Tiwaz, and Thurizaz has a similar action energy – a very direct one.

My wife and I got married on a day that suited our natal charts. I try as much as possible to get my books released on good energy days, and I launch products and courses on days that are filled with the energy I want them to be. I'm not saying that the cosmos does the work for me, far from it, but acting in alignment with its energetic flow does make life much easier.

I talked about consulting the gods earlier and it's useful to know how often they move through the runic zodiac, so you can plot where they'll be. See below:

God	Runic Zodiac Time
Sunna	About 15 days
Manni	About 1.25 days
Odin	About 7 days
Freya	About 14 – 18 days
Tyr	About 25 days
Thor	About 180 – 190 days
Loki	About 1.25 years
Urõr	About 3.5 years
Njord	About 7 years
Myrmir	About 7 – 15 years

Table 6: Gods/Planets in the Runic Zodiac

Finally, I want to make sure you realize this is more than just rune maths and planet maths. It's trusting your intuition, your insight and your heart. Trust your feelings as you build Runic Star Paths for yourself, your events or your clients. This is where power is to be found. Right there. In you. Your heart will lead you to victory.

Have fun using runic astrology for love, business, wealth, happiness, or whatever you choose.

You've come searching and have started on the path. The goddesses and gods have noticed. Their gaze is upon you.

Afterword

Once you've opened the door to the mystic, it does not close. And now you've activated power within yourself that the gods and goddesses cannot fail to notice. Even though you're probably not wearing copper armour and standing on a hilltop shouting, 'Hey, Odin!', you may well find that the powerful one-eyed one turns that baleful eye towards you. Or the queen of the heavens raises an eyebrow in your direction. Maybe if you're super unlucky (or privileged?), the bobbing head in the cave will bless you with a sneer.

Whatever energy casts its eye over you, by reading this book you've accessed a frequency of the *Wyrd*, the Norns have spun more power into your specific thread of destiny and you have gained the power to navigate and co-create your next steps in ways that you may not have even imagined before you started reading.

You want proof? You've just read it. I am not an astrologer, but I was and am keen to learn. I learned the lore and sang the songs. And the universe moved to make it so, from getting my *very* patient editor on side, to the CEO of the company signing off on it, to my wife patiently loving me, suggesting ideas and correcting my errors, again and again and again, to being here now, sharing this with you.

My life's *Wyrd* has changed since I started reading and interpreting Runic Star Paths. Yours will too if you choose to act on the frequencies that are drawn to you and through you.

You have already begun to learn the lore. You have begun to feel the energy of the songs. You are now walking your Runic Star Path – a path that has lain forgotten and decayed for far too long, a path that is now becoming activated by fresh new footprints, a path that you can walk along and leave your mark on in whatever way you choose.

Be ready to become more and more of yourself as you navigate these times.

You've chosen this. Embrace it.

I've mentioned before that gods will take an interest in you as you work with the runes. Let me finish this with a small story that illustrates this.

As I was finishing editing this book, I went to Normandy with my wife.

If you don't know Normandy, it was named after the settlers that came from Norway in the ninth century. They spent lots of time raiding and settling along the big French rivers, and left their marks all over Europe.

In Rouen, Hrolf the Walker was the first Norman count. Hrolf is a Norwegian name, and when Latinized by the Franks became Rollo. Rollo's home became Rouen.

We got to Rouen on Wednesday, Odin's day. And after a frustrating drive around the city trying to find our way to the hotel, we dumped the car and went exploring.

Rouen is a medieval city, with cobbled streets, ancient buildings and massive churches. It's also where Jeanne d'Arc was held before her execution. That's its own story, and not one for me to tell here.

If, like me, you are interested in how people's ideas of the divine evolve, then this may be of interest. When the pagan Northmen became Christian Normans, the Church turned Odin into St Cnut, and Thor into St Olaf. And surprisingly in this very Christian church in Rouen we found a shrine to St Olaf. I'd not seen one outside Scandinavia, though to be honest, I'd not looked too hard, so that was a surprise. He even had a Viking longship in his shrine. And a relic of the saint. The description was stamped in brass in a dark corner and I couldn't get at it to read it, but just the fact that it's there is quite cool. I lit a €2 candle to St Olaf and we made our way to the church of Jeanne d'Arc.

This is a church built in the 1970s on the site of her execution. It's meant to look like a wave. To me, it looks like a longhouse from Norway, but that's just how I look at things.

This flowing building has a massive burning sword sculpture in its grounds and is surrounded by medieval buildings, once wattle and daub, mud and straw, but I suspect now painted brick and plaster. People throng around the ancient marketplace, with street hawkers, police and beggars everywhere.

As we entered the church, down a surprisingly narrow concrete corridor, there was a beggar at the door. As with most of the beggars I'd met, I ignored him. As I'd previously learned, if not, you get swamped by people asking for money.

He greeted Lisa as she passed and gave me a derogatory snort. I glanced up, and saw a surprisingly strong and lean body clad in a worn leather jacket, faded jeans and worn army boots, and a ragged face, lined with the years, a salt-and-pepper beard and, what knocked me back, one eye, the other scarred over, as if from a blade or other wound.

I paused, but the push of tourists forced me through the doors and into the church.

To say I was a little shaken would be an understatement. I sat on the edge of a pew while Lisa explored. Looking back, I couldn't see where the beggar was standing.

As I sat looking at the altar, made in the image of flames, I realized that I hadn't honoured the, to me, quite blatant incarnation of the All-Father.

I went back out to find him, but he was nowhere to be seen. Instead, there were a lot of police, obviously doing a sweep of the 'undesirables' in the area. I wandered the area, poked my head in alleyways and watched as the police chased groups of people away from the tourist hotspot.

Then I saw him. I approached him and made my offering. He looked at me, nodded and disappeared into the crowd.

Feelings that I'd been pondering for a while came and went as I waited for Lisa to finish her investigations.

And that, dear friend, is how I met Odin in Rouen. And knew he was taking an interest in how I was moving through the world. So, dear walker of the Runic Star Path, be ready for when the gods take notice of you. Because they will.

CLOSING RITUAL

꩜≪◈≫꩜ ⋯◇≫◈⋯X≪○≫X⋯◈≫◇⋯꩜≪◈≫꩜

You'll need:

• a candle

• two drinking vessels

• a drink of some sort

• your journal

Ritual is the cornerstone of developing your connection to runic astrology. So, to close this book and to continue your journey into ancient runic knowledge, I invite you to honour the energy of the one-eyed god who brought the knowledge of the runes to humankind, or indeed to honour any goddess, god or energy that draws your vibration.

There are many ancient rituals that have been lost to the sands of time and others that don't fit with the ethics of the current time. One that has persisted and remains suitable is that of honouring others by sharing food and drink with them. So...

• Find yourself a still space. I know that may not be easy with life going on and children and partners demanding your time, but take a few quiet moments for yourself and the gods.

+ In your quiet space, lay out your journal and two drinking vessels. I've a couple of Viking drinking horns, but then I'm a purist (or perhaps pedant). Wine glasses, tumblers or even sippy cups work.

+ Pour yourself a generous measure of your favourite drink. I use mead (see, purist!), but wine, beer, juice and squash are all fine. And pour an equally generous measure into the other vessel.

+ If you feel comfortable, then light a candle. Again, as I'm anal, I have beeswax ones. But tea lights work well, or even tallow if you're going for the full ancient experience!

+ With your journal in front of you, take three deep breaths slowly in through your nose and out through your mouth, one for each of the Norns. As you exhale, let your shoulders relax and give your jaw a wiggle.

+ Either out loud or internally, say:

> *Norns, gods and goddesses of the cosmos, thank you for guiding me on this path. I offer you this drink to honour your wisdom.*

+ Sip, glug or otherwise consume your drink. And allow some time for any energetic shifts you may feel. They may be super subtle.

- When you have finished your drink, take the gods' drink and use it to water the plants or drink it yourself. Don't just pour it away, as there is energy in it.

- Tidy up and ready yourself. This is the end of this book and you have opened portals, pathways, to the Wyrd and the cosmos. Remember to journal what you feel, dream and experience. These feelings are uniquely yours and have power.

Go forth, create Runic Star Paths for yourself, your friends, your dog. Explore and create magic, mystery and power.

They are yours by right.

Own them.

Big love,

Rich xxx

Acknowledgements

I'd like to give deep love and appreciation to my radiant and powerful wife, Lisa, without whose insight and guidance I'd not be half the man I am today. And this book would not exist.

Thanks to Jon, Paul, Andy, Seb and Dylan and the Scouts at 1st Fareham for your tolerance of all the times I've missed sessions and your patience as I've brain-dumped on you during this process.

To Kay and Ron, Masie, Megs, Tilly, Buffy and Blaze, and the sheep, ducks, chickens, and goose (probs not the goose, you are a git), for providing a place to manifest ideas and create awesomeness in darkest Aquitaine.

To Kezia and the kitten, for your patience.

About the Author

Richard Lister is a trained nurse, intuitive body worker, life coach and spiritual guide. He works with clients globally, offering one-to-one sessions, workshops and online coaching, and specializes in embodiment, spiritual resilience and personal connection. Rich is made from the stuff of Vikings. His interest in all things Norse began at the age of four and he has been reading and working with the runes for 20 years.

 www.richardlister.com

 @richlisteruk

CONNECT WITH
HAY HOUSE
ONLINE

 hayhouse.co.uk   **f** @hayhouse

@hayhouseuk   @hayhouseuk

@hayhouseuk   @hayhouseuk

Find out all about our latest books & card decks • Be the first to know about exclusive discounts • Interact with our authors in live broadcasts • Celebrate the cycle of the seasons with us • Watch free videos from your favourite authors • Connect with like-minded souls

'The gateways to wisdom and knowledge are always open.'

Louise Hay